A Table Full of Welcome

A Cookbook

Celebrating Kansas City's culinary diversity

by Doug Worgul

★ KANSAS CITY STAR BOOKS

A Table Full of Welcome
Celebrating Kansas City's culinary diversity

Written and edited by Doug Worgul
Photography by Talbott L. Wilson
Book design and production by Kelly Ludwig

Published by KANSAS CITY STAR BOOKS
1729 Grand Boulevard
Kansas City, Missouri, USA 64108

First edition

Library of Congress Control Number: 2002090958

ISBN: 0-9717080-2-9

Printed in the United States of America
By Walsworth Publishing Co.

To order copies call StarInfo, (816) 234-4636

For more information about this and other fine books from
Kansas City Star Books visit our Web site at www.thekansascitystore.com.

Table of Contents

When I arrived here in Kansas City 14 years ago, one of the things I liked first and liked best about this place was its ethnic diversity.

I moved here from Kalamazoo, Michigan, a mid-sized upper-Midwestern town where the largest ethnic group was Dutch. My own ethnic background — if you can call it that — is German and English, and in practice it's not much different than Dutch. As a result, I always felt comfortable in Kalamazoo, but rarely challenged or curious or entertained or enlightened. I was aware of and enjoyed encounters with Kalamazoo's other ethnic populations. But, at least when I lived there, the city was so remarkably homogeneous that, well, it was kind of like having a nice helping of mashed potatoes — with not quite enough gravy — for dinner everyday.

In comparison, I have found Kansas City to be a rich stew, brimming with big tasty chunks of exotic ingredients and unfamiliar flavors.

I like strolling the aisles of my grocery store and hearing three or four different languages spoken by the time I leave. I like it that people in my own neighborhood dress differently than me, knowing that their clothing is an outward expression of cultures that evolved under the influence of geography, religion, invasions, migrations and traditions different than those that shaped my own culture.

Most of all, I like eating the food that comes from cultures different than my own.

This cookbook celebrates Kansas City's culinary diversity. It invites you to dinner with eight Kansas City families, representing eight different ethnic groups. And then it invites you to make some of their food in your own kitchen.

Of course, there are far more than eight ethnic groups represented in Kansas City. But for reasons of cost and practicality, eight will have to be enough for now. Perhaps we can explore the food traditions of another eight another time.

There are four things that should be understood about the recipes in this book. First, these are not my recipes. I did not invent them and I claim no ownership of them. Most of these recipes are at least many decades, perhaps centuries, old. These recipes are like folk legends and fairy tales, told and retold through the ages. The origins and authors of these recipes are, for the most part, unknown. They represent the folk food traditions of ancient cultures and have been passed down within communities and families from generation to generation. My role in presenting these recipes is not that of author but of researcher, tester, taster, transcriber, adapter and editor.

Next, these recipes are not to be followed. Not exactly. I rarely follow a recipe exactly. And I don't expect you to. In fact, I encourage you not to. The recipes in this book are starting points from which you may go in many directions. They are melodies upon which you may improvise, creating your own harmonies of flavors and textures.

Third, if a recipe in this book doesn't work for you, don't give up on it. Change it. Try it again another way. Change it until it tastes and looks the way you want it to.

Finally, there are a couple of things missing from these recipes that are typically included in other cookbooks. You will notice first that I do not specify yields for these recipes. Yield estimates annoy me. I find them to be of little or no value. How many people a recipe serves depends on a wide variety of variables, including the ages, sizes, genders, appetites and moods of your guests. Most experienced cooks can safely gauge, based on the measurements in an ingredients list, how many people will be fed by any given recipe under any given circumstances. So use your own judgment. I trust you.

Another thing missing, in most instances, are specific measurements for salt and pepper. The use of salt and pepper is highly subjective. Use amounts that suit you.

I do, however, recommend that you use kosher salt whenever possible and practical. It tastes better and is easier to use in most recipes. And always use freshly ground pepper. It tastes better and it's fun to grind.

In a very real way this book belongs to the eight families who extended to me their gracious hospitality in allowing me a seat at their tables: the Brownes, the Willises, the Krizmans, the Tans, the Medinas, the Red Corns, the Fingershes and the Avellutos. These families welcomed me with great warmth — which inspired the title of the book — and they will always have my sincere gratitude.

I am also grateful to the following for their help in creating this book: Ruth Baum Bigus for referring me to the Fingersh family; Jose Bayani for referring me to the Tan family; and Suzanne Lozano for referring me to the Medina family.

My deepest thanks to Talbott L. Wilson for his gorgeous photographs, and to Kelly Ludwig for her elegant design.

This book is dedicated to my wife, Rebecca. I would be neither a writer nor a cook without her. It is also dedicated to my daughters, whose help and presence in the kitchen has always been a joy; and to my father-in-law, Ben, who has always liked my cooking.

— Doug Worgul
Kansas City, 2002

Irish Traditions

*"The process of making the food is as
important as eating it.
That's when you put all the love in."*

The Irish are the world's best storytellers. Irish stories and the poets, novelists, playwrights and barstool raconteurs that tell them, set the standard to which the rest of the world's storytelling is compared.

Kerry Browne, co-owner of Browne's Deli in Kansas City and as Irish as a shamrock, says that in Ireland there are two things to aspire to: to tell a good story and to make a good scone.

There is, it seems, a connection between the two. In fact, food is a primary theme in many Irish stories.

An early Irish fable features a cauldron that feeds the entire nation and yet remains full. Another old folktale tells of 80 pots overflowing with porridge, to the delight of hungry villagers. One mythic Irish hero is a guy dubbed Dagda of the Huge Appetite.

And in the ancient Irish epic, "The Feast of Bricriu," the main character devotes an entire year to preparing a banquet for his friends — and his enemies. These preparations even include the building of a mansion expressly for the purpose of housing dinner guests.

Left: Nellie Feehan and Riley. Above: Margie Browne and Ginny Cleary.

Ireland is a small island nation located off the west coast of Great Britain. It is only a little more than 300 miles long and about 170 miles wide — slightly larger than our state of West Virginia. Because of its proximity to and shared history with Britain and Europe, Ireland's culinary history has been significantly influenced by British and European cooking traditions. It has, however, developed some unique food traditions of it own.

As an island nation, fish has obviously been a part of the traditional Irish diet, though not to the extent one might assume. Farm livestock have actually played a much more important role. Anthropologists say that medieval Irish texts reveal that cattle and diary products have been central to Irish cooking for centuries. Even more important, has been the role of the hog. Bacon, hams, sausages and roasted pork have been fundamental in Irish cooking for more than a millennium.

In these tales, warriors, foreigners and even tricksters up to no good are offered milk and bread — without a second thought - whenever they are in need of it.

These stories reveal the hospitality fundamental to Irish identity. In ancient Irish society, strangers were offered food and drink before they were asked to declare the nature of their business. To withhold hospitality was not only a serious breach of etiquette, but also a punishable crime.

This trait of gracious generosity is summed up in a line of dialogue from an old Irish legend: "My finest meats and wines are yours!" Which could also be the motto of Kerry Browne's family.

For more than 114 years the Brownes have welcomed Kansas City to their unique store at 33rd and Pennsylvania. This charming little place, which started out as a corner grocery and butcher shop, is these days an Irish eatery, a packaged gourmet goods store and a purveyor of fine Irish gifts.

And while the Browne's are in the business of selling, not giving away, their food and drink, hospitality is nevertheless their main stock-in-trade. Even if you're a Kowalski and not an O' Quigley you'll be warmly received by the Brownes.

This is as true in their homes as in their store.

One of Ireland's most cherished culinary traditions is its whiskey. When England's King Henry II invaded Ireland in 1170, he found several commercial distilleries producing whiskey.

It is the potato, however, for which Irish cooking is most known. Sir Walter Raleigh is said to have introduced the potato to Ireland, though this has never been verified. Whenever and by whomever potatoes arrived, they soon became essential to Irish cooking and have remained so since.

By the mid-19th century, the potato had, in fact, become so important in Ireland's diet and economy that when the potato crop failed due to an infestation of blight, a devastating famine resulted that changed the course of Irish and American history.

The Irish refer to the potato famine as "The Great Hunger." It resulted in starvation and death on a scale unheard of in a modern Western nation. Between 1840 and 1860 1.7 million Irish immigrated to the United States to escape the effects of the famine and to start a new life.

Many of these immigrants came to Kansas City, if only as a stopover on their way to some other place. But a few stayed. And then a few more. And then thousands more. By 1990, according the U.S. census, people of Irish ancestry made up Kansas City's single largest ethnic group.

Ed and Mary Flavin, immigrants from County Kerry, Ireland, founded the little store now known as Browne's Market, in 1887. In 1901, they bought the property on the southwest corner of 33rd Street and Pennsylvania Avenue where the deli now stands. They paid $1,150.

The store was on the first floor and the Flavins lived upstairs. Their daughter and son-in-law, Margaret Flavin Browne and James R. Browne Sr., assumed ownership of the store in 1917 and changed the name to James R. Browne Grocery.

James R. "Bob" Browne, Jr. married Margie Blake in 1955 and two years later he and his wife bought the business. When Bob Browne died in 1981, their daughter, Kerry Browne and her business partner — now husband — John McClain, took over the operation.

Some of the information in this story came from interviews conducted by The Kansas City Star's Joyce Smith

John McClain puts the finishing touches on the trifle.

Conor Feehan, who may someday be as fine a cook as his Aunt Kerry.

Not long ago, I was invited to dinner at the home of John and Deb Feehan. Deb's maiden name is Browne and she and her husband and children are an enthusiastic and active part of her sister Kerry's business. When I arrive, I am greeted at the door by the Feehans' overly gregarious puppy, Riley, who has eluded the grasp of Nellie Feehan, Deb and John's teen-age daughter. Nellie has as bright an Irish face as you'll ever see.

Riley escorts me into the kitchen where final dinner preparations are under way and appetizers are being served.

John McClain, Kerry Browne's husband and business partner, pours me a Guinness stout. Kerry is at the stove, stirring a pot of rutabagas.

"Help yourself to a sausage roll," she says. "And then be sure to have some of the smoked salmon on brown bread. You know, most folks think it's called brown bread because of its color. But really they named it after us. It should be spelled 'browne bread' — with an 'e' at the end."

This is my first taste of smoked salmon on browne bread and my first taste of Kerry Browne's gentle wit. There will be plenty of both this evening.

Kerry is putting the finishing touches on her version of the traditional Irish favorite; shepherd's pie. "In Ireland," she says, "the process of making food is as important as the eating of it. That's when you put all the love in it."

Kerry adds an extra bit of grated cheese to the top of the pie.

The kitchen soon fills with family and friends. John Feehan's parents, Phil and Joann, arrive, followed by friend Ginny Cleary and Sister Virginia Browne, Kerry's and Deb's aunt, who is a nun in the order Sisters of St. Joseph, Carondelet. The decibel level increases precipitously. Nellie's siblings, Shannon, Conor and Ryan clamor through, grabbing hands full of sausage rolls on their way.

Margie Blake Browne, Kerry's mother and the matriarch of the clan, speaks up from the adjacent family room, where she's been chatting with her son-in-law, John Feehan. "This is the way we Irish like it," she laughs. "Chaotic."

The Brownes and Feehans are first and quite thoroughly American. Yet their Irishness is a conscious and integral part of their identity. It's more profound than the simplistic ethnic pride displayed on bumper stickers ("Kiss me, I'm Irish"). It is as much a part of the way they define themselves as gender or religion.

Kerry, her husband, John and her mother, Margie, visit Ireland at least once a year for reasons both personal and professional.

"We go over there to maintain relationships with vendors. But it also keeps us connected to our family there," Kerry says. "It keeps us connected to the traditions and frankly, to the changes taking place in Irish society. It's not the little fairy tale country people imagine it to be. It's a real and vibrant part of modern Europe."

John nods in agreement.

"As much as Ireland has progressed in the last 20 years, its culture is still very much rooted in tradition," John says. "Especially in the countryside. That's where we get ideas for many of the culinary events we host at the store."

As family members gather around the Feehan's dining room table, I ask Deb how often the extended family gets together to eat.

"Actually we get together at Mom's house every Sunday," she says. "All families should do that. It keeps you together."

Margie shakes her head and sighs. "So many people don't have time anymore for the things that really matter."

We are served a rich vegetable soup, a flavorful puree of carrots and parsnips, a delightful rutabaga casserole, a hearty beef roast and — my favorite — shepherd's pie. It is all wonderful.

But it's apparently not enough for Margie.

"Where's the corn fritters?" she wants to know.

Kerry laughs. "Well, Mom, you didn't make them, so we don't have them."

When I ask if corn fritters are Irish in origin, the answer is definitive.

"We always made corn fritters for our family dinners and we're Irish," Margie states. "Therefore fritters must be Irish."

This is a family prone to easy laughter and gentle kidding.

Kerry teases her sister, claiming the only way Deb is able to recall a particular family event is by remembering what was eaten at the time. Wasn't that when we had that great pineapple cake?

Deb turns it right around. "Hey, sometimes the food is the only memorable thing about our family get-togethers."

When dessert is served it occurs to me that this will be a most memorable evening, both for the food and the company.

Kerry has made quaint golden little queen cakes, a fruit cake fragrant from the Irish whiskey that has been poured on top of it and a splendid trifle that is almost too pretty to eat.

The four Feehan children have all lined up for helpings of dessert. I ask if any of them have an interest in cooking, and Nellie and Conor smile and say they do. Conor, who seems always to be smiling, informs me that he has recently graduated from making plain grilled cheese sandwiches and is now perfecting cheese and chicken quesadillas. He says, however, that pancakes are his specialty.

Sister Virginia, who is seated next to me and who declined dessert in favor of coffee, eyes the trifle on my plate. She leans toward me. As she asks, "Do you mind?" she scoops a big spoonful of whipped cream from the top of my dessert and in one smooth motion plops it in her drink. She takes a sip. "Thank you," she says.

As the children begin to clear the plates, Kerry raises her glass for a traditional Irish toast. "Go Mbeirimid beo ar an am seo aris," she says in Gaelic. "May we all be here this time next year." To which, I am told, the appropriate response is "Good Lord willin'."

Browne Family Recipes
and other traditional Irish dishes

Mary Ann O'Shea's Vegetable Soup

A wee bit o' butter or oil
  for sautéing
3 potatoes, peeled and diced
1-1/2 yellow onions, chopped fine
2 carrots, peeled and chopped
1 parsnip, peeled and chopped
1 stalk celery, chopped,
  including leaves
4 cups chicken stock

1 cup milk, heated
1 cup peas (frozen are preferred
  over canned)
1 bunch green onions, chopped
Salt
Pepper
Thyme
Poultry seasoning

You may substitute with other vegetables you have on hand. Root vegetables work best. In a stockpot, sauté potatoes, onions, carrots, parsnip and celery in the butter or oil until well coated. Season with salt, pepper and thyme. Cover over low heat for 10-12 minutes, stirring occasionally. Add chicken stock. Boil for 15 minutes — not too long or the vegetables will lose their flavor. Put mixture in a blender and puree. Return to the pot and add warmed milk, peas, green onions and dash of poultry seasoning. Heat through. For thicker soup, use cream instead of milk.

Champ

1-1/2 lbs. potatoes, cleaned, skin
   on, cut in pieces
6 scallions, chopped fine
1-1/4 cups milk
Butter
1/4 cup sour cream
Fresh parsley, chopped
Salt
Freshly ground pepper

Boil potatoes in salted water just until tender. Drain the potatoes by pouring the hot water over the chopped scallions. In a saucepan, bring the milk and the blanched scallions to a boil. Add the cooked potatoes and season with salt and pepper to taste. Mash with potato masher. Stir in sour cream. Top with butter, more chopped scallions and chopped parsley.

P.J.'s Rutabagas

2 large rutabagas
1 thick slice good lean salt pork,
   about the thickness of your
   finger (can use thick slab
bacon if you can't find
   salt pork)
Freshly ground pepper

Boil the salt pork in water about 20-30 minutes while you are preparing the rutabagas. Peel all the thick skin off the rutabagas and slice medium-thin. Put them in the water with the salt pork and reduce heat. Cook over low heat for about another hour or until tender. Top with plenty of pepper. The cook eats the salt pork, or you can cut it up and add to the rutabaga.

Kerry Browne at work at the stove.

Marge's Mashed Carrots and Parsnips

These are great reheated in the microwave the next day so make extra.

6 carrots, peeled and chopped
3 parsnips, peeled and chopped
1 onion, quartered
1/2-3/4 cup milk, heated

2 tbsps. butter, or more
Salt
Pepper

Boil vegetables in salted water. For flavor, add quartered onion, leaving the pieces big enough that they can be removed later. Cook veggies until tender. Drain well. Remove onion. Add warmed milk and butter. Mash with potato masher. Add salt and pepper to taste. The liquid may separate out a bit so stir before serving. Top with a little bit more butter.

Mary Hickey's Beef Roast

4-5 lb. rump roast
4 carrots, peeled and cut in
    2-inch pieces
6 potatoes, quartered and boiled
1 large yellow onion, quartered
1 large can stewed tomatoes,
    drained

Whole grain Guinness mustard
Salt
Pepper
Thyme
1/2 bottle Guinness stout
1/2 cup water

Preheat oven to 350 degrees. Line roasting pan with heavy tin foil. Add roast. Rub the top with whole grain mustard salt, pepper and thyme. Top with tomatoes and onions. Place remaining onions and carrots around roast. Add 1/2 bottle Guinness and 1/2 cup water to pan. Drink remaining half bottle of Guinness. Cover pan with a foil tent. Cook 20 minutes per pound, or until internal temp has reached at least 160 degrees. Add cooked potatoes and allow roast to brown by cooking uncovered for the last 20 minutes. Use broiler at end if roast isn't brown enough. Use pan drippings to make Bisto gravy.

Bisto Gravy

Bisto is Ireland's favorite gravy mix. Kerry Browne says she even sprinkles
Bisto granules in her homemade gravy "just to make it taste more like home."

For each cup of gravy:
Bisto granules
1 tbsp. meat drippings or butter

1 tbsp. flour
1 cup beef stock or water

Over medium-high heat, bring drippings or butter to a bubble. Gradually stir in flour to make a roux. Continue stirring for about a minute or two, being careful not to let it burn. Gradually add stock, then bring to a boil. Let boil for about a minute then reduce heat. Add Bisto granules to taste. (NOTE: Adding Bisto will thicken your gravy, so you may want to make adjustments by adding or reducing the amount of stock you use.)

Margie's Corn Fritters

1 can corn (Margie prefers
    Green Giant© brand)
About 1/2 cup milk
1-1/2 cups flour
3/4 tsp. salt

1/4 tsp. sugar
3 tsps. baking powder
1 egg
Vegetable oil

Drain corn, reserving liquid. Add milk to corn liquid to make 1 cup. In a medium mixing bowl, beat the egg into the milk mixture and add the corn back in. Sift together the dry ingredients, then gently mix these into the milk and corn mixture until just moistened. In a small skillet, into which you have poured about 1 inch of vegetable oil, gently drop a heaping tablespoon of batter and fry on medium high heat. Brown on each side. If your oil is too hot the fritters won't cook through. The cook gets to eat the first fritter to make sure it's properly done. Drain. Serve plain or sprinkled with powdered sugar or cinnamon sugar. Great for a special breakfast or as a side dish with chicken dinner.

White Dinner Soda Bread

Kerry recalls her grandmother admonishing her, "Don't overwork the dough or it'll be tough!"

4 cups flour
1 tsp. salt
1 tsp. baking soda

1 tsp. sugar (optional)
2 cups buttermilk

Preheat oven to 450 degrees. In a large mixing bowl, sift together dry ingredients. Add buttermilk to flour mixture. Lightly knead dough with your fingertips. Don't overwork the dough or it'll be tough. Form a round loaf on a lightly floured pie pan (Kerry prefer tins, but glass will do). Cut a cross in the top with a floured knife, to let the evil spirits out. Bake on the top rack for 35-40 minutes. When baked properly, the loaf will have a hollow sound when tapped on the top. Wrap in a tea towel after removing from the oven to prevent the loaf from getting too crusty.

Brown(e) Bread

1-1/4 cups white flour
2-1/2 cups whole wheat flour
1/4 cup bran (if you don't like bran,
    substitute one of the flours)

1 tsp. baking soda
1 tsp. sugar (optional)
2 cups buttermilk

Prepare as you would the white soda bread, above.

Tralee Shepherd's Pie

2 lbs. ground chuck	Freshly ground pepper
4 carrots, scrubbed and shredded	Garlic powder
2 large yellow onions,	Seasoned salt
chopped fine	Parsley
1 cup frozen corn	Green onions
1 cup frozen peas	Shredded cheddar or other
5 cups mashed potatoes	yellow cheese
Salt	

For the gravy:

1 can Bisto	1 tbsp. tomato paste
	A wee bit o' red wine

In a heavy skillet, brown ground beef with chopped onion, salt and pepper. When nearly done, add shredded carrots and continue browning evenly. Drain fat from beef and carrots on paper towels, then return to skillet. Stir in peas and corn and set aside.

Preheat oven to 325 degrees.

In separate pan, make Bisto gravy following instructions on label (if Bisto is not available, make your favorite beef gravy). Add the tomato paste, red wine, fresh ground pepper, a dash of garlic powder, and a dash of seasoned salt. The gravy should be fairly thick to hold the beef and vegetable mixture together. If it's not thick enough, make a roux with flour and butter and stir it in. Mix the gravy with the meat mixture and spoon into 2 pie pans or a casserole dish. Top with your favorite mashed potatoes, spreading the potatoes evenly over the entire top. Cover with foil. (At this point, the dish may be kept in the refrigerator for up to two days.) Bake for about 30 minutes. Remove foil and sprinkle with chopped parsley, chives and a little more shredded cheese. (The green, the orange, and the white symbolizing the Irish flag.) Return to the oven until cheese is melted. Let cool about 10 minutes before serving. Great with brown bread.

Gertrude Boland's Fruit Trifle

Bishop Boland is a dear family friend. This recipe was his mother's.

1 stale sponge cake (may be made a few days ahead and left uncovered until needed)	1 jar good raspberry jam
	3-4 cups whipping cream
	Powdered sugar
1 package lady fingers	Vanilla extract
1 can peaches, drained	A few fresh strawberries
1 can pears, drained	Slivered almonds-lightly roasted
(reserve liquid)	1/4 cup good sherry
1 bag frozen strawberries, thawed and partially drained	(not cooking sherry)

Line the outside of a straight-sided glass bowl or trifle dish with standing lady fingers that have been spread with raspberry jam, jam side in. Slice sponge cake thin (as for a torte), spread with jam and place in bottom of bowl. Top with a thin layer of peaches, pears and a bit of the frozen strawberries. Repeat with another layer of cake and fruit, cutting and piecing as necessary to make layers fit nicely. Take the reserved pear juice and sherry (totaling about 1/2 cup; use more or less to your taste) and pour over layered cake and fruit. Cover and refrigerate overnight (or at least 3 hours). Prepare whipping cream; add a bit of vanilla and powdered sugar at the end of the whipping process. Top the trifle with the cream, then garnish with slivered almonds and cut fresh strawberries. Serve chilled in pretty glass dishes.

The following are not Browne family recipes, but are reflective of traditional Irish and Irish-American cooking.

Traditional Irish Stew

3-lb. boneless lamb shoulder, trimmed and cut into 1-inch pieces
1-1/2 tbsps. fresh parsley, chopped
1 tsp. dried thyme
6 cups chicken stock
3 lbs. potatoes, peeled and quartered

1 large onion, chopped fine
1 lbs. carrots, peeled and cut into 1/2-inch pieces
6 stalks celery, cut into 1/2-inch pieces, include leaves
6 tbsps. flour
1/4 cup vegetable oil
Salt
Freshly ground pepper

In a large stockpot, add the lamb, parsley, thyme, salt and pepper to taste and 4 cups stock. Bring to a boil, then reduce heat, cover and simmer for 1-1/2 hours. Then add potatoes, onion, carrots, celery and remaining 2 cups stock. Bring back to a boil, reduce heat, cover and simmer for another hour. In a small bowl whisk together flour and oil until smooth. Add this to the stew and stir until completely incorporated. Remove cover and continue to cook for another few minutes as the broth thickens. Season with salt and pepper.

Sausage Chowder

8 cups chicken stock
1 lb. Irish sausages, diced
1 medium yellow onion,
    chopped fine
1 cup finely diced carrots
2 cloves garlic, minced

3 cup raw potatoes, diced
Salt
Pepper
2-3 cups heavy cream
Grated sharp cheese
Chopped scallions

In a stockpot cook the diced sausage and onions until both are nice and brown. Add the chicken stock, carrots, potatoes and garlic, season with salt and pepper and bring to a boil. Reduce heat and let simmer until potatoes are just tender. Stir in heavy cream until desired consistency is achieved. Serve with grated cheese and chopped scallions on top.

Split Pea Soup

1 lb. dried split peas (choose the
    yellow split peas if you can
    find them)
8 cups chicken stock
1 cup diced ham
1 cup finely diced carrots
1 medium yellow onion,
    chopped fine

2 cloves garlic, minced
1/2 tsp. rubbed sage
Salt
Pepper
Bacon fat (or butter)
Sour cream

Sort and rinse dried split peas. In a stockpot, cook the peas in the chicken stock until quite tender. Remove from heat and let cool. Remove peas with a sieve, leaving the stock in the pot. In a food processor, puree the peas and set aside. Bring the stock to a boil, add the diced ham, carrots, garlic and sage. Reduce heat and cook until carrots are tender. In a small skillet cook the chopped onions in a bit of bacon fat (or butter) until the onions have begun to caramelize. Add pureed peas and onions to the stock, season with salt and pepper and bring back to a boil. Serve with a dollop of sour cream on top.

Rebecca's Potato Soup

8 cups chicken stock
4 cups mashed potatoes
2 cups raw potatoes, diced
2 cups sour cream
1 large yellow onion, chopped fine
1 lb. bacon, chopped fine

Salt
Freshly ground pepper
2 cups grated cheddar cheese
    (Kerry Gold, if you can find it)
1 cup chopped green onions

Cook the chopped bacon and onion until the bacon is nice and crisp and set aside. In a large stock pot, bring the chicken stock to a boil, add raw potatoes, reduce heat and cook potatoes until just tender. Stir in mashed potatoes, then sour cream, bring back to a boil. Add bacon and onion mixture, saving back enough bacon bits to sprinkle a few on top of soup when served. Salt and pepper to taste. Serve topped with grated cheese, chopped green onions and bacon bits.

Kale and Cream

2 lbs. kale	1/2 tsp. nutmeg
2 cups pearl onions, peeled	Salt
6 whole cloves garlic, peeled	Pepper
2 tbsps. butter	1/4 cup beef stock
1 cup heavy cream	

Start a stockpot with boiling salted water.

Wash the kale under cold running water. Trim leaves from stems. Using tongs, push the kale into the boiling water and cook with the pearl onions and whole garlic cloves until tender, 20-30 minutes. Drain thoroughly and chop fine. In a saucepan combine the butter, cream, nutmeg and salt and pepper to taste. Then add the kale and the beef stock. Stir until the sauce is slightly reduced. Serve warm.

Bacon and Cabbage

1 large head cabbage	Pepper
8 strips bacon	4 whole allspice berries
Salt	3 cups chicken stock

Preheat oven to 350 degrees. Core and quarter the cabbage, then boil in salted water for 15 minutes. Drain and soak in ice water for one minute. Drain again and slice the cabbage thin. Put four of the strips of bacon on the bottom of a medium-sized baking dish. Cover with the cabbage. Season. Add only enough stock to cover the cabbage, then top with the remaining strips of bacon. Bake uncovered for about an hour. Cover with foil if the top begins to get too brown.

Rutabaga Pudding

I lb. rutabagas	I tsp. sugar
3 tbsps. bread crumbs	I tsp. ginger
I cup heavy cream	I egg and 2 egg yolks, slightly
2 tsps. butter, melted	beaten
I tsp. salt	

Preheat oven to 350 degrees. Clean, peel and cube the rutabaga, and boil until tender. Drain. Mash thoroughly in a mixing bowl; then add remaining ingredients. Blend well. Pour into a 9-by-9-inch baking dish and bake for 1 hour. Serve warm.

Stout Potato Salad

6 medium potatoes, peeled and cubed	Freshly ground pepper
8 slices bacon, chopped fine	2 tbsps. butter
I small red onion, chopped fine	2 tbsps. flour
2 cloves garlic, minced	3 tbsps. sugar
2 carrots, diced	8 oz. Guinness stout
Salt	3 tbsps. cider vinegar

Boil potatoes, garlic and carrots in medium-size saucepan until just tender. Drain and set aside in a large bowl. In a small skillet cook chopped bacon and onion until bacon is crisp. Melt butter in a small saucepan, then gradually add flour and stir until blended and smooth. Add sugar. Slowly stir in beer and vinegar. Bring to a boil, stirring constantly. Pour over potatoes. Toss lightly and let stand 1 hour. Add bacon and red onions; toss gently and serve.

Potato Pancakes

I cup raw potatoes, peeled and grated	Milk
I cup mashed potatoes	I egg
I cup flour	Salt
	Pepper

Grate raw potatoes and mix with the cooked mashed potatoes. Add flour and salt and pepper to taste. Beat egg and add to mixture with just enough milk to make a batter that will drop from a spoon. Drop by tablespoonfuls onto a hot griddle or frying pan. Cook over medium heat for 3-4 minutes on each side.

Kerry Browne and her shepherd's pie.

Stout Pie

1-1/2 lbs. ground sirloin	1 tbsp. raisins
1/2 lb. bacon, chopped	5 medium yellow onions,
2 tbsps. flour	chopped fine
Salt	1 bottle Guinness stout
Pepper	Pie crust (see below)
1 tbsp. brown sugar	

Cook the bacon and onions in a heavy skillet or pot over medium heat until bacon begins to brown. Add ground sirloin and continue cooking until beef is crumbly and thoroughly browned. Turn heat up and cook a bit longer until onions caramelize. Stir in flour, then add brown sugar, raisins and salt and pepper to taste. Add about half a bottle of Guinness, cover and simmer over low heat for about an hour, adding more stout as needed when the sauce gets too thick.

Line a pie dish with half the piecrust. Bake it empty until just beginning to turn golden, about 10 minutes: then add the meat mixture. Cover with the top piecrust. With a sharp knife, make a few slits in the top crust, then bake another 10 minutes, or until top crust is golden brown.

For the pie crust:

1 cup cold butter	4 cups flour
6 tbsps. cold lard	1 tsp. salt
(or vegetable shortening)	10-12 tbsps. ice water

This pie dough may be made well ahead of time and refrigerated until use.

In a large chilled mixing bowl, quickly work the cold butter and lard into the flour using your fingertips, until the mixture is crumbly. Turn flour mixture onto work surface and make a little indentation or "well" in the middle of the top of the flour pile. Add the ice water to this well, stirring into the flour mixture with your fingers in a quick but gentle swirling motion, moving from the middle out. Using your fingertips work the water and flour mixture into a dough. Do not overwork. Wrap tightly in plastic wrap and chill for at least 2 hours before using. May be kept in refrigerator for up to a week before use.

Divide the dough into two equal parts. Make a ball with each half. Then, using a pastry cloth and a rolling pin stocking and a little flour on your work surface, roll each ball of dough into a disk about 1/8-inch thick. Roll from the center to achieve uniform thickness.

Lamb Chops with Herb Butter and Creamy Caramelized Onion Sauce

8 lamb chops

For the sauce:
12 yellow onions,
    sliced paper thin
8 tbsps. olive oil

1 tbsp. sugar
1 cup dry white wine
Salt
2 cups heavy cream

In a large heavy skillet, sauté the sliced onions in the olive oil over medium-high heat until they are golden brown and beginning to caramelize. This will take awhile and it will seem at first as if there are way too many onions. But when they cook down they will lose more than 2/3 of their original volume. When the onions have browned up nicely, add the sugar, a pinch of salt, and the white wine, lower heat and reduce the sauce. Stir in the cream about five minutes before serving, stirring constantly bring to a boil and immediately remove from heat.

For the herb butter:
1 lb. cold butter
3 large leaves spinach,
    chopped fine
4 large leaves sweet basil,
    chopped fine

3 leaves fresh sage, chopped fine
3 sprigs fresh mint, chopped fine
2 cloves garlic, minced
1/2 tsp. salt
1/2 tsp. white pepper

Add all ingredients to a food processor and pulse until just blended. Remove to a glass bowl, cover and chill until time to serve.

Grill lamb chops over and charcoal fire. Use apple chunks in your fire for extra flavor. When done, spoon about 2/3 cup (or more) onion sauce on a warm plate. Place a lamb chop on top of the sauce, and serve with a tablespoon of herb butter on top of the chop. Serve with cold potato salad or with mashed potatoes.

Ham with Whiskey Sauce

4 large ham slices
1 small yellow onion, chopped fine
1 tbsp. brown sugar
1 tbsp. whole-grain mustard
2 tbsps. Irish whiskey

3 tbsps. flour
2 tbsps. butter
3/4 cup beef stock
Salt
Pepper

Fry ham in butter over medium-high heat in heavy skillet for about 7-8 minutes each side (before frying, snip fat around the edges of each ham slice, to prevent curling).

To make the sauce, remove ham slices and cook onions in the pan butter until beginning to caramelize. Gradually stir in flour. Add stock, then sugar and bring to a boil. Lower heat and simmer for about 2 minutes, stirring constantly. If sauce is too little thick, add a bit more water. Remove from heat. Add whiskey, mustard and season to taste. Serve ham with sauce.

Margie Browne, Nellie Feehan and Deb Feehan. Deb is Margie's daughter and Nellie's mom.

Corned Beef and Cabbage

My research for this book leads me to believe that this dish is more popular here in the States as a St. Patrick's Day meal than it is in Ireland itself. But you were, no doubt, expecting it, so here 'tis.

1 lb. kosher salt	1 bunch carrots, peeled and cut
1 gallon water	into 2-inch pieces
2 tbsps. pickling spice	1 large turnip, peeled and cut
1 brisket (7 to 8 pounds)	into 2-inch cubes
6 whole bay leaves	2 medium yellow onions,
10-12 black peppercorns	quartered
8 whole cloves	8 large potatoes, peeled and
1 large head cabbage, cored	halved
and quartered	

Mix salt, water and pickling spice in large stainless steel stockpot. Put your brisket in the pot, refrigerate and cure for at least 48 hours. NOTE: The brisket needs to be completely covered, so make a sufficient amount of brine. After 48 hours, remove brisket. Dispose of brine and thoroughly rinse stockpot. Return brisket to pot and cover with fresh water. Add bay leaves, peppercorns and cloves. Cover and bring to a boil. Reduce heat, cover, and cook over medium-high heat 3 to 3-1/2 hours or until fork-tender. During last 45 minutes of cooking time, add cabbage, carrots, onions, turnip and potatoes. Remove meat to serving platter and let rest for about 15 minutes before serving.

Irish Risotto

*Yes, I know. Risotto is an Italian dish. However, if you use some distinctly Irish ingredients,
you come up with a distinctly delightful Irish variation on the theme.*

2 cups steel-cut oats
6 tbsps. butter
1/4 small yellow onion,
    chopped fine
1/2 head green cabbage, sliced
    thin, then chopped fine
1 cup sliced mushrooms
1 tbsp. sugar

2 cloves garlic, minced
5-6 cups chicken stock
2 tbsps. fresh parsley,
    chopped fine
1/2 cup grated Blarney cheese
Salt
Pepper

Bring chicken stock to a boil. Heat butter in heavy saucepan over medium-high heat. Add onion, cabbage and mushrooms. Sauté over medium-high heat for about 10 minutes. Be careful not to let the butter get too hot. Stir in the oats and sauté for about 5 minutes, until oats are well coated. Add sugar, then garlic. Then add hot chicken stock one cup at a time, stirring continuously, until each cup of stock has been absorbed by the oats. When oats are rich and creamy in texture, with a bit of bite left, remove from heat. Stir in parsley and cheese. Season with salt and pepper. Serve hot.

Apple and Barley Pudding

1 cup pearl barley
1-1/2 lbs. Granny Smith apples,
    peeled, cored and sliced
1/2 cup sugar
1/2 tsp. cinnamon

1/2 tsp. nutmeg
1 tsp. grated lemon peel
1 tbsp. fresh lemon juice
Heavy cream

Bring slightly salted water and barley to a boil. Add sliced apples and simmer until the barley and apples are soft. Remove from heat and let cool. Blend thoroughly in a food processor and return to the saucepan. Add sugar, cinnamon, nutmeg, lemon juice and lemon peel. Bring to a boil again. Remove from heat; allow to cool. Pour into a serving bowl and chill completely. Serve cold with heavy cream.

Apple Rhubarb Crisp

2 cups rolled oats
1 cup brown sugar
3/4 cups flour
1/2 tsp. nutmeg
2 tsps. cinnamon
1 tsp. salt
1/2-3/4 cup butter, melted

3 cups Granny Smith apples,
   cored, peeled and sliced
2 cups rhubarb, sliced
1/4 cup granulated sugar
1 tbsp. fresh lemon juice
Whipped cream

Preheat oven to 400 degrees. In a medium bowl, combine the rolled oats with the brown sugar, flour, 1-1/2 tsps. of cinnamon, nutmeg and salt. Add melted butter and mix until evenly moistened. Work the mixture with your fingers forming large crumbs. In a bowl, combine the apple slices, rhubarb, granulated sugar, lemon juice and remaining 1/2 tsp. of cinnamon. Spread the fruit mixture in 9-by-9 baking dish. Spread the oatmeal crumb topping over the fruit. Bake for about 30 minutes, or until the fruit mixture is tender, the filling is bubbly and the topping golden-brown. Serve warm with whipped cream. A little sugar and a splash of whiskey in the whipped cream wouldn't hurt.

Porter Cake

1 cup porter beer
1 cup butter
1 cup brown sugar
6 cups mixed dried fruit
   (equal quantities currants,
   raisins, dried apricots and
   dried pineapple)
4 cups flour

1/2 tsp. baking soda
1/2 tsp. cloves
1/2 tsp. cinnamon
1/2 ginger
Grated rind from one small
   lemon
3 medium eggs, 3 egg yolks

Preheat oven to 325 degrees. In a saucepan combine the butter, sugar and porter. Over medium heat melt butter and sugar. Add fruit and simmer for 10 minutes. Set aside and let cool. Add the flour, baking soda, spices and lemon rind and combine. Beat the eggs and stir them into the mix with a wooden spoon. Pour into a greased 9-inch cake pan and bake for about 1 hour 45 minutes. Use the toothpick method to test the cake for doneness. Let the cake to cool in the pan. Serve with whipped cream (see recipe above regarding sugar and whiskey).

African-American Traditions

*"Soul food is comfort food. Because of the
way it tastes and the way it makes you feel.
It brings to mind home, good times, and
Sundays after church."*

Even the wisest poets and preachers find it difficult to
describe *soul* — that indefinable depth of character
and character of depth that can't be learned or bought, only achieved. If
you've got soul, you know it. If you don't, you don't. Soul can't be seen or
touched. But it can be felt. And, at the table of Lavell and Vera Willis, it
can be tasted.

The soul food Vera Willis cooks is as savory as memory, as sweet as
celebration, as salty as sadness and as spicy as family.

I am welcomed to the Willis home with warmth and graciousness.

"Make yourself comfortable," says Lavell, extending his hand.
"Hope you're hungry!"

He proceeds to introduce me to those of his four children and 16
grandchildren who are on hand for the evening's meal. The heady aroma of
fried chicken, collard greens, sweet potato pie, and peach cobbler fills the
Willis house, distracting me from my journalistic tasks. I put down my

Left: Vera Willis and daughter-in-law Aundral Wilmore. Above: Rian Wilmore, Vera's granddaughter.

While the phrases "soul food" and "Southern cooking" are not precisely synonymous, they overlap considerably.

The English, Scottish and Irish settlers who arrived in the New World in the 17th century obviously brought with them the culinary traditions of the British Isles. But conditions on the North American continent were harsh, food was scarce, and these traditions had to be quickly adapted to a new reality.

The indigenous peoples living along the Eastern Seaboard were proficient at growing corn and this soon became critical to the survival of the European newcomers. The settlers learned from the natives how to cultivate corn and traded with them for the corn they needed beyond that which they could grow. Corn has been an integral part of Southern cooking ever since, used in everything from succotash, to grits, to cornbread, to whiskey.

The Europeans who settled in what is now the American South brought with them cattle and pigs and potatoes, and these have remained a part of Southern cooking. The settlers also brought with them African slaves. And while slavery will forever be a source of profound shame for the American nation, the contributions of African slaves to American culinary traditions are something to celebrate.

Native African foods such peas, okra, eggplant, peanuts and yams were brought to this country by slaves and were quickly and permanently integrated into the diet of the American South.

Since slaves were required to do the cooking for their owner's entire household, African cooking techniques were also soon inextricably incorporated into Southern food traditions.

In Louisiana, where Vera Willis was born and raised, there were significant additional influences that shaped a unique regional style of Southern cooking. French settlers brought their stews and soups. Spanish settlers introduced onions, peppers, garlic (the "holy trinity" of Louisiana cooking) and tomatoes. Slaves added African spices and okra. And Indians contributed indigenous foods such as crawfish, shrimp, oysters, crabs and pecans into the local cuisine.

Some of the information in this article came from research conducted by students enrolled in Dr. Terry Prewitt's 1996 Applied Anthropology class at the University of West Florida, Pensacola.

notebook and head straight for the kitchen, where Vera is clearly queen.

"This is all good Southern food," she says. "We used to eat like this more often before life got so busy. Eating in the South is a lot more social than it is in other places. With Southern food you don't eat and run, you sit and eat. And you socialize."

Vera and her husband, Lavell, are very busy these days. They are the proprietors of the Peach Tree Buffet, a successful soul food restaurant on Kansas City's East Side. And while they may not themselves have the time to sit and relax and eat as often as they'd like, the Southern food they serve has attracted a diverse clientele of satisfied customers, few of whom seem to be in any hurry to leave the table.

Owning and operating a restaurant was a dream for both Lavell and Vera, even before they met and married. Vera's father was a restaurateur in Oak Grove, Louisiana. He was also a Methodist bishop and tomato farmer. Lavell's father was in the restaurant business in Fresno, Californian, where Lavell grew up.

"Louisiana is more known for its style of soul food than any other state in the nation," says Vera. "So I guess I it's natural that I love to cook."

Lavell nods. "First thing I learned when Vera and I got married was that in Louisiana you eat when it's offered. If you don't they can get mighty offended."

Vera says that opening the Peach Tree has been the highlight of her professional life. "I enjoy serving people," she says. "I enjoy seeing people enjoying our food. Both my customers and my employees call me 'Mom' and that's a nice thing."

One of the things Vera and Lavell like best about their restaurant is that its clientele comprises people from all races and ethnic backgrounds. "Some days I'll notice that there are more white folks in the dining room than black folks," Vera says. "Soul food is simply old-home cooking, down-home cooking. When I first opened the restaurant, I didn't think white folks would eat this food — collard greens, sweet potato pie, neck bones. But they do. And they like it. That's because they know it's made with lots of love and respect for tradition."

"That, and it tastes good," says Lavell.

"Soul food is comfort food. Because of the way it tastes and the way it makes you feel," Vera states." It brings to mind home, good times and Sundays after church."

And maybe it's church and Bible reading and prayer that make the

Erin and Rian Wilmore. Below: Reggie Wilmore, Vera Willis' son, and his daughter, Taylor.

Willises' soul food more soulful than just anybody's. They seem to have made God a full partner in their business from Day One.

"I even prayed that God would send me a name for the restaurant," recalls Vera. "The Peach Tree Buffet is the name he sent."

Lavell sighs. "I was planning on calling it 'Lavell's' or 'Lavell's Place', but how can you argue with God?"

The Peach Tree first opened its doors on a Saturday afternoon in 1996. The Willises were pleasantly surprised with their first day's business. But the success of their first day was immediately surpassed by the triumph

Vera Willis enjoys the conversation at her dinner table.

of their second day. At about 2 o'clock that afternoon, Lavell panicked when he saw the long line of hungry people extending out the restaurant door, around the building and out into the parking lot. He was sure they would run out of food and end up with a mob of angry people on their hands. He had to think quickly and act fast.

And so he did.

"I solved our problem, dear," he told Vera, who was working away in the kitchen. "I locked the door."

His wife stared at him in disbelief. "You go right out there and unlock that door," Vera demanded.

And so he did.

And it all turned out all right. "I don't think anybody went hungry," says Lavell.

"I think so," says Vera.

If anybody did go away hungry that day, nobody has since. The buffet-style service at the Peach Tree pretty much guarantees that all customers leave satisfied.

Jason Hawkins, a supervisor at the restaurant, is the Willises' godson. He says his godparents are tough-minded when it comes to business, but tender-hearted with their employees.

"They've given me and a lot of other young people some great opportunities," he says. "They're firm but fair. They're great examples to us. We all look up to them."

The affection is mutual.

"We've known Jason since he was 14," Lavell says. "He started working for us the day after he turned 15. He's 20 now and he's a valuable part of our operation and our family."

It's not always easy to be gracious and generous in the restaurant business. It's hard to attract and keep good workers, and the profit margins are thin. "It's a tough business," Vera points out. "It's tough physically, mentally and emotionally. And if you're not careful and you're not good at what you do, it can be very tough and unforgiving financially. But this restaurant is my ministry. I try to apply bibical principles to my business just as I do in my personal life."

One of the early challenges for Vera was achieving consistency in the food served at the Peach Tree. "Many of the folks I hired to work in the kitchen were good cooks," Vera says. "But they were what I call 'dump cooks.' They weren't used to measuring their ingredients. They'd just dump a little of this and a little of that in the pot and taste-test as they went along."

Which is all fine and good for cooking at home. But, as Vera explains, it's no way to run a restaurant kitchen. Folks expect that each time they come to a restaurant and order a dish it'll taste the same as it did the last time.

"That's why I had to retrain all my cooks at the Peach Tree," she says. "I had to get them to use the same recipes each time, every time.

"To be honest with you, I'm something of a 'dump cook,' too," she confesses. "And now I'm used to preparing food in such large quantities at the restaurant that it's hard for me to remember how to cook for just my family."

Cooking for family seems to be the guiding philosophy at the Peach Tree.

"We try to treat each of our guests as if they were coming to eat in our home," Lavell says.

In fact, many of the restaurant's regular customers have become part of an extended Willis "family" over the last six years.

"Not long ago one of our good customers had some serious health problems and had to be hospitalized over in St. Louis," Lavell recalls. "Well, we were concerned about him, so we called to the hospital just to check on him, see how he was doing. Well, his family was there, and they just couldn't believe that we'd care that much about him. But we did. And we do. It's how we've chosen to conduct our business."

Vera nods in agreement. "This restaurant is my ministry. I try to apply Biblical principles to my business just as I do in my personal life."

Hospitality is one biblical principle the Willises most definitely adhere to. As I busy myself with my heaping plate of food, I begin to worry that Vera will wear herself out doting on me. Have I had enough chicken? Did I try the neck bones? Am I ready for some peach cobbler? Chareka, dear, please get our guest some more iced tea.

And it's all wonderful. The black-eyed peas are earthy, pungent and filling. The chicken is crispy and perfectly seasoned on the outside, tender and juicy on the inside. And the sweet potato pie tastes like a holiday.

"So?" I ask. "Can a white guy like me learn to make soul food?"

Vera considers my question for a moment.

"Why, yes, I do believe you could," she concludes. "You could, if you made it in your heart as well as in your kitchen."

Chareka Wilmore helps her grandmother, Vera, in the kitchen.

Willis Family Recipes
and other traditional African-American dishes

Down-Home Fried Chicken and Southern Gravy

*One of Vera's fondest memories is the aroma of her mother's chicken,
deep fried in a black cast-iron skillet.*

1 whole frying chicken cut in pieces (8-10 pieces)	1/4 tsp. paprika
1 cup flour	1/2 tsp. garlic powder
1/4 tsp. seasoned salt	1 cup vegetable shortening

Rinse chicken thoroughly in cold water. Heat shortening in skillet or electric frying pan to 365 degrees, or medium-high. Combine flour and seasoning in a large plastic bag and shake well. One at a time, shake chicken pieces in the bag with the seasoned flour. Carefully put chicken in the skillet and fry on both sides until crispy and golden brown, about 30 minutes. Drain on paper towel before serving.

Option: Marinate rinsed chicken pieces in buttermilk for a few hours before coating with seasoned flour.

To make gravy, drain all the grease from the skillet into a saucepan. Leave all the little brown pieces in the skillet. For each cup of gravy you wish to make, return 2 tbsps. of grease to the skillet. (If you need four cups of gravy, you'll need 8 tbsps. of grease.) Turn heat under the skillet to medium high. Then for each 2 tbsps. of grease in the skillet, gradually stir in 2 tbsps. flour to make a roux. Stir until smooth and bubbly, scrapping the little brown bits off the bottom of the pan. Then gradually add one cup of milk for each cup of gravy, the first cup being a can of evaporated milk. (If you're making four cups of gravy, you'll need one can of evaporated milk and three cups regular whole milk.) Bring to a boil and let bubble for 1 minute then remove from heat. Salt and pepper to taste. Serve with mashed potatoes.

Vera usually serves iced tea with her traditional Southern fare.

Southern Fried Catfish

4 catfish fillets, about 9-12 oz. each
1 cup yellow cornmeal
1 tbsp. seasoning salt
1 tsp. garlic powder
1/4 tsp. onion powder
1/4 tsp. paprika
2 cups canola oil

These are best when cooked in a cast-iron skillet. Butterfly each fillet by cutting it in half lengthwise, but all the way through. In a medium mixing bowl, combine cornmeal, seasoning salt, garlic powder, onion powder and paprika. Preheat canola oil in skillet to 350 degrees, or medium high. Coat fillets on both sides in cornmeal mixture. Fry until golden brown, about 3 to 5 minutes on each side.

Fried Potatoes and Onions

6 medium white potatoes,
  peeled and sliced
2 medium yellow onions,
  chopped medium

1 cup canola oil
2 tsps. seasoning salt
1 tsp. white pepper
2 tsps. garlic powder

Preheat canola oil in skillet or electric frying pan to 350 degrees. Place potatoes, onions, seasoning salt, white pepper and garlic powder in skillet. Cover and cook until potatoes are fork tender and golden brown. Turn potatoes and onions frequently with a spatula to prevent sticking.

Jalapeno Hushpuppies

1 cup yellow cornmeal
2/3 cup all-purpose flour
2 tsps. sugar
1 tsp. salt
2 tsps. baking powder
2 eggs
3/4 cup whole milk

2 tbsps. canola oil
3/4 cup finely chopped onions
1/2 cup chopped jalapeno
  peppers
2 cups canola oil or enough
  to cover hushpuppies
  when cooking

In a medium mixing bowl, mix all dry ingredients. In a large bowl, stir eggs, milk and 2 tbsps. oil together. Gently fold the dry ingredients into the milk and egg mixture. Add onions and peppers and stir. Preheat canola oil in deep fryer or frying pan to 350 degrees. Drop the batter in rounded teaspoons full into preheated oil and cook 2-3 minutes on each side or until golden brown.

Black-eyed Peas

2 lbs. dried black-eyed peas
2 smoked ham hocks
1 large yellow onion, chopped fine
4 cloves garlic, chopped

1 tbsp. sugar
Salt
Freshly ground pepper

Thoroughly sort and wash peas. In a large stockpot, cover the peas with twice as much cold water as there are peas and let soak overnight. The next day, drain and rinse the peas and set aside. Fill the stockpot with plenty of cold water, then add the ham hocks, onions, garlic, sugar, salt and pepper. Bring to a boil, reduce heat and let simmer for an hour or two. Add the peas, adding more water if necessary, bring back to a boil, reduce heat and let cook until peas are tender. May be served over rice.

Healthy Greens

Vera is concerned about the incidence of high blood pressure and heart disease among African-Americans and so she has devised this low-fat version of greens, a traditional soul food favorite.

2 bunches fresh greens, such as
    collards, turnip, mustard
    or mixed
2-1/2 quarts chicken broth
1/2 yellow onion, chopped fine

1 clove garlic, minced
1/8 tsp. salt (optional)
1/8 tsp. white pepper
1/8 tsp. thyme
Nonstick vegetable cooking spray

Thoroughly wash, rinse and trim stems from greens. In a large stockpot, cover the greens with chicken broth and bring to a boil. Reduce heat and cook until tender. Do not overcook. Remove from heat and drain greens well. Retain broth, as this may be used as the base for soups or stews. Spray a large skillet with nonstick vegetable cooking spray and place over medium heat. Add onions, garlic and thyme. Cook until onions are translucent. Add drained greens and 1/4 cup of the chicken broth. Cook until liquid has evaporated. Serve hot.

Okra and Tomatoes

1 cup fresh or frozen cut okra
1 cup fresh or canned diced
    tomatoes
1 cup water or tomato juice

1 tbsp. butter
1 tbsp. salt
1 tsp. pepper
1 tbsp. Original Mrs. Dash

Preheat oven to 350 degrees. Mix all ingredients in a small casserole dish, cover and bake for 30 minutes or until okra and tomatoes are tender. Avoid over-stirring.

Fried Okra

10 okra pods
1 cup yellow cornmeal
1 tbsp. flour
1-1/2 tsps. seasoned salt

1/2 freshly ground pepper
1/4 tsp. paprika
Bacon drippings

Cut okra in 1/4-inch slices. Sprinkle with cold water. Blend dry ingredients. Dredge okra in seasoned cornmeal mixture until well coated. In a heavy skillet, melt bacon drippings over medium-high heat. Fry okra in bacon fat until golden brown. Drain okra on paper towel and serve.

Candied Yams

6 sweet potatoes, scrubbed
1 cup brown sugar
1/4 cup water
1/2 cup butter

Pinch nutmeg
1 tsp. fresh lemon juice
2 tsp. vanilla extract

Preheat oven to 350 degrees. In a large saucepan, boil potatoes for about 10 minutes, until just fork-tender. Drain and fill pan with cold water to facilitate cooling. When potatoes are cool enough to handle, peel and cut potatoes in 1/2-inch-thick slices lengthwise. Place slices in a buttered baking dish and dot with butter. In a small saucepan, bring brown sugar, water, vanilla, nutmeg and lemon juice to a boil. Pour over potato slices. Bake uncovered 45-50 minutes, basting frequently with syrup.

Rian Wilmore

Peach Cobbler

1 cup sugar
3 tbsps. cornstarch
1/4 tsp. cinnamon
1/4 tsp. nutmeg
3 (15 oz.) cans canned peaches
2 tbsps. butter
1 cup flour
2 tbsps. sugar

1-1/2 tsps. baking powder
1/2 tsp. salt
1/3 cup butter
1 egg, plus two egg yolks
1/4 cup milk
2 teaspoons pure vanilla extract
1 tbsp. sugar

Preheat oven to 375 degrees. Combine one cup sugar, cornstarch, cinnamon and nutmeg in large bowl. Add peach slices and toss to coat. Grease 8-inch square pan with butter and add peaches. In a medium bowl, whisk together the flour, 2 tbsps. sugar, baking powder and salt. Cut in the 1/3 cup butter until coarse crumbs are formed. In a small bowl beat the egg and yolks. Add the milk and vanilla and mix well. Combine milk mixture with flour mixture until flour is just moistened. Don't over-mix. Drop batter by large spoonfuls onto the peaches. Sprinkle 1 tbsp. sugar over the batter. Bake for 25-30 minutes or until cobbler is golden brown.

Kathy Price's Quick & Easy Deep Dish Peach Pie

This recipe is from Vera Willis' sister.

Pie pastry for top and bottom
Deep dish pie shells
Two (16 oz.) cans yellow cling
    peaches in heavy syrup

1/4 cup brown sugar
3 tbsps. sugar
1 tbsp. real vanilla extract
1 stick butter

In a large saucepan combine the peaches (with syrup), brown sugar, sugar, vanilla and butter. Cook over medium heat for about ten minutes, until mixture begin to thicken. Preheat oven to 350 degrees. Line a deep dish pie pan with pie pastry and spoon in peach mixture, including some of the syrup. Don't over saturate. Cover with top pie crust. Pinch top and bottom crust together. With a sharp knife make a few 1-inch slits in top crust. Bake for 35-40 minutes, until top crust is golden brown.

Pie Crust

1 cup cold butter
6 tbsps. cold lard
    (or vegetable shortening)

4 cups flour
1 tsp. salt
10-12 tbsps. ice water

This pie dough may be made well ahead of time and refrigerated until use. In a large chilled mixing bowl, quickly work the cold butter and lard into the flour using your fingertips, until the mixture is crumbly. Turn flour mixture onto work surface and make a little indentation or "well" in the middle of the top of the flour pile. Add the ice water to this well, stirring into the flour mixture with your fingers in a quick but gentle swirling motion, moving from the middle out. Using you fingertips work the water and flour mixture into a dough. Do not over work. Wrap tightly in plastic wrap and chill for at least two hours before using. May be kept in refrigerator for up to a week before use.

Divide the dough in two equal parts. Make a ball with each half. Then using a pastry cloth and a rolling pin stocking and a little flour on your work surface, roll each ball of dough into a disk about 1/8-inch thick. Roll out from the center to achieve uniformity of thickness and shape.

Big Momma's Bread Pudding

4 cups toasted bread, torn or
    cut in pieces
1 quart whole milk
1-1/2 sticks butter, melted
1-1/2 tsps. vanilla extract
4 eggs

3 cups sugar
1 tsp. salt
1 tsp. nutmeg
1 tsp. cinnamon
1 tbsp. baking powder

Preheat oven to 350 degrees. In a large mixing bowl thoroughly combine eggs, butter, sugar, salt, nutmeg, cinnamon, vanilla and baking powder. Stir in milk. Add bread and stir to coat. Pour into a buttered baking dish or casserole and bake for 1 hour or until pudding no longer jiggles when the pan is shaken gently. Cover with foil if top begins to get too dark.

For the sauce:

2 cups whole milk
1 tbsp. cornstarch
2 eggs, slightly beaten

1-1/2 cups sugar
1 tbsp. vanilla extract
1/4 tsp. nutmeg

Combine all ingredients in a medium saucepan. Cook over medium heat, stirring continuously until the mixture thickens to the consistency of heavy cream. Serve warm over Big Momma's Bread Pudding. (Bread pudding may also be served with Caramel Bourbon Sauce, Page 51.)

The following are not Willis family recipes, but do reflect African-American cooking traditions as well as the increasing popularity of African-influenced dishes.

Super Creamy Macaroni and Cheese

1 16 oz. package elbow
    macaroni, cooked
1 package (8 oz.) regular (not
    low-fat) cream cheese
4 cups shredded extra-sharp
    cheddar cheese
1 stick butter
8 tbsps. flour

1 cup half-and-half
3 cups milk
1/2 tsp. salt
1/2 tsp. white pepper
1/2 tsp. garlic powder
1/2 tsp. onion powder
1/2 tsp. dry mustard

In a large saucepan, melt butter. Over medium-high heat, gradually stir in the flour. Stir until smooth and bubbly. Let bubble for about 1 minute. Gradually stir in half and-half and milk. Stirring continuously, bring to a boil. Let boil for one minute. Remove from heat and add cream cheese, cheddar cheese and seasonings. Stir thoroughly. Add cooked macaroni and mix until all the macaroni is well coated. May be served at this point. Or pour into a buttered casserole, top with some more shredded cheddar and bake for 30 minutes or until cheese on top is melted and beginning to brown.

Green Beans and Red Potatoes

6 lbs. fresh green beans	2 medium yellow onions,
3 lbs. red potatoes, scrubbed	chopped fine
and quartered	Salt
2 lbs. bacon, chopped fine	Freshly ground pepper

In a heavy skillet, cook bacon and onions until both are brown and crisp. Trim the ends of the green beans, cutting the longer beans in half. In a large stockpot, boil beans in salted water for about an hour. (This will make the beans much softer than most culinary school-trained chefs recommend. But this is "comfort food," as Vera Willis reminds us, and soft beans are comforting.) With about 15 minutes of cooking time remaining, add potatoes and continue cooking until potatoes are just fork-tender. Drain. In a large serving bowl combine the beans, potatoes, bacon and onions. And if quite a bit of the bacon fat also finds its way in there...oh well. Salt and pepper to taste. Serve warm.

Skillet Cornbread

1-1/2 cups cornmeal	1/2 cup boiling water
3/4 cup flour	1-1/2 cups buttermilk
2 tbsps. sugar	2 large eggs, beaten lightly
1 tsp. salt	3 tbsps. melted butter
2 tsps. baking powder	3 tbsps. melted bacon grease
1/2 tsp. baking soda	

Preheat oven to 425 degrees. Put 1 tbsp. of bacon grease in a well-seasoned 9-inch cast-iron skillet and put the skillet in the oven while preheating. Sift together 1 cup of cornmeal and the remaining dry ingredients. In a large bowl mix the buttermilk, eggs, butter and remaining bacon grease. In a small bowl, pour 1/2 cup boiling water over 1/2 cup cornmeal and mix to form mush (this will look like grits). In the large bowl thoroughly combine the mush with the wet ingredients. Add the dry ingredients and combine until the flour mixture is just moistened. Don't over-mix. When the oven is heated to 425, remove the skillet and pour in the batter. Return skillet with batter to oven and bake for 25 to 30 minutes. Use the toothpick method to check for doneness. Serve warm with butter, honey or maple syrup.

Green Bean Salad with Lemon Peanut Dressing

1 lb. fresh green beans
4 tbsps. peanut oil
1 small red onion, halved then
    sliced thin
2 cloves garlic, minced
1/2 cup dry roasted peanuts
1/2 cup creamy peanut butter

2 tsps. fresh rosemary,
    chopped fine
2 tsps. fresh lemon juice
Pinch cayenne pepper
Salt
Freshly ground pepper

Bring enough salted water to cover green beans to a boil in a large pot. Fill a large bowl or pan about half-way with ice water. Trim the ends of the green beans and put them in the boiling water. Cook for about three minutes, until beans are still crisp, but slightly more tender than raw. Drain the beans in a colander, then plunge the green beans into the ice water and stir to stop the cooking process. Drain and set aside.

In a food processor, blend oil, peanut butter, garlic, rosemary, cayenne and lemon juice. Pour over green beans and toss with red onions and peanuts.

African Squash, Yams and Peanuts

Many African-Americans have begun to include in their diets traditional dishes from the African continent as a way of celebrating their heritage.

1 small yellow onion, chopped
    into 1-inch pieces
2 tbsps. peanut oil
2 medium yams or sweet
    potatoes, peeled and cubed
2 cups acorn squash, peeled
    and cubed

1 cup coconut milk
1/2 cup unsweetened coconut
3/4 cup dry roasted peanuts
1/2 tsp. salt
1/2 tsp. ground cinnamon
1/4 tsp. cloves

In a heavy skillet sauté onion in oil over medium heat until tender. Stir in remaining ingredients. Bring to a boil. Reduce heat, cover and let simmer for about 10 minutes. Remove cover and let simmer for a few minutes longer until vegetables are tender.

Jason Hawkins is a supervisor at the Peach Tree Buffet and a frequent guest at his godparents' house.

Fried Yams or Sweet Potato Fries

In Nigeria and other West Coast African nations, fried yams are popular.
Sweet potato fries are popular in many Kansas City barbecue joints.
That makes this recipe a natural African American-style treat.

6 sweet potatoes, peeled
Peanut oil
1/4 cup sugar
1 tsp. paprika
1 tsp. seasoned salt

1 tsp. onion salt
1 tsp. garlic powder
1 tsp. cayenne pepper
1 tsp. chili powder

In a mixing bowl thoroughly blend sugar and spices. Adjust to taste. Cut sweet potatoes lengthwise in french-fry-style strips about 1/4-inch wide. In a heavy skillet, an electric frying pan or deep pot, pour about 2-3 inches of peanut oil and heat to medium-high. In small batches, fry sweet potato fries until crispy on the outside and soft on the inside. Adjust heat up or down as necessary. While fries are still hot and glistening, sprinkle with the seasoning mix. While these fries are delicious as is, they're also tasty with catsup or barbecue sauce.

Red Beans and Rice

This dish is a favorite in Vera Willis' home state of Louisiana.

1 lb. dried red beans
2 lbs. smoked sausage, diced
1 smoked ham hock
1 large yellow onion, chopped
1 stalk celery, chopped,
    include leaves
1 green bell pepper,
    cored, seeded, chopped

3 cloves garlic, minced
1 tsp. dried thyme
Freshly ground pepper
Salt
Cayenne pepper and/or your
    favorite Louisiana-style hot
    sauce
Freshly cooked white rice

Sort and thoroughly rinse beans, then soak overnight in cold water. Drain and rinse beans. In a large stockpot add all ingredients except rice. Cover with plenty of water. Season with salt, pepper and cayenne to taste. Bring to a boil, then reduce heat and simmer for 2-3 hours, until beans are tender. Season again if necessary. Remove approximately 1/4 to 1/2 cup beans and mash to a paste. Stir this paste back into the beans and cook for about 15 more minutes. Serve over rice.

West Coast African Beef Stew

2 lbs. stew meat, cubed
4 cups beef stock
1 (28 oz.) can stewed tomatoes,
    undrained
1 green bell pepper,
    cut in 1-inch pieces
1 stalk celery, cut diagonally,
    include leaves.
1 medium white potato, cubed
1 large carrot, sliced diagonally

1 medium yellow onion, cut in
    half, then sliced thin
1 sweet potato, peeled and cubed
4 cloves garlic, chopped
1 tsp. salt
Freshly ground pepper to taste
6 tbsps. tomato paste
1/2 teaspoon cayenne pepper
1 cup chunky-style peanut butter

In a stockpot, combine beef, beef stock, tomatoes, bell pepper, celery, potato, carrot, onion, garlic, sweet potato, salt, pepper and tomato paste. Mix well. Bring to a boil; reduce heat. Cover and simmer for about an hour, adding more if necessary. Stir in cayenne pepper and peanut butter. Simmer for another hour or until vegetables and beef are tender. Serve over rice.

Kenyan Vegetable Pot

2 large onions, chopped fine
2 tbsps. peanut oil
1 tbsp. cumin seeds
2 tsps. mustard seeds
8 medium potatoes, peeled
    and quartered
1-1/2 tsps. fresh ginger, grated
4 cloves garlic, minced
1 tbsp. ground cumin
2 tsps. coriander
1 tsp. cayenne pepper

1/2 tsp. turmeric
1 tsp. salt
1 tsp. cinnamon
6 whole cloves
4 oz. tomato paste
1/2 lb. fresh green beans, trimmed
1 medium eggplant, diced
Florets from one head of broccoli
1 bunch of greens, such as kale,
    spinach or collards
1 cup canned chickpeas

Preheat oven to 350 degrees. In a large, heavy skillet or ovenproof pot, over medium high heat, sauté the onions and the cumin and mustard seeds in the oil. Add the potatoes and coat well with oil and toasted seeds. Add seasonings and continue to stir for several minutes. Stir the tomato paste into the pot and then add about a cup of water to thin the tomato paste a bit. Add vegetables one at a time, cooking for a couple of minutes before adding the next batch of veggies. Add the chickpeas last. Cover skillet or pot with lid (or foil) and bake for about 45 minutes.

Aundral Wilmore and daughter, Taylor.

Caribbean Chicken

1 roasting chicken, skin removed,
    cut into pieces
2 tbsps. apricot preserves
4 green onions, chopped fine
4 cloves garlic, chopped fine
1 tsp. cayenne pepper

1 tsp. salt
1/2 tsp. black pepper
1/4 cup fresh lime juice
1 tsp. lime zest, finely chopped
1 tsp. curry powder
1 tbsp. soy sauce

In a mixing bowl combine apricot preserves, onions, garlic, cayenne pepper, salt, black pepper, lime juice, lime zest, curry powder and soy sauce. Mix well. Season chicken pieces with salt and pepper, then rub each piece thoroughly with Caribbean seasoning. Place in a covered plastic container and marinate in the refrigerator for about an hour. Bake covered for 1 hour at 400 degrees.

West African Jollof Rice

2 cups water
3 lbs. chicken pieces
2 (15 oz.) cans stewed
    tomatoes, including liquid
1 large yellow onion, sliced thin
1 cup cooked smoked ham, cubed
1 cup uncooked rice

3 cups cabbage, shredded fine
1/2 lb. fresh green beans, trimmed
    and cut in 1-inch pieces
1/4 tsp. ground cinnamon
1/4 tsp. cayenne pepper
Salt
Freshly ground black pepper

In a large stockpot, add the water, chicken, onion and tomatoes (with liquid). Season with salt and pepper. Cover and bring to a boil, then reduce heat and simmer for about 30 minutes. Add ham, rice, cabbage, green beans, cinnamon and cayenne. Bring back to a boil, then reduce heat and simmer, covered, until the chicken is fork-tender and the rice is cooked, about 30 minutes.

Lavell Willis entertains his granddaughters Rian and Erin with a story.

Sweet Potato Pie

Vera Willis' Methodist minister father may not have approved, but I think adding a little bourbon to this pie makes it special.

1 9-inch pie shell, partially baked
2 lbs. sweet potatoes (about 4-5 medium potatoes)
2 tbsps. unsalted butter, softened
3 large eggs, plus 3 yolks
1 cup sugar
1/2 tsp. nutmeg
1/4 tsp. salt

2-3 tbsps. bourbon or rye
1 tbsp. maple syrup or molasses
1 tsp. vanilla extract
2/3 cup whole milk
1/4 cup brown sugar (for sprinkling on the bottom crust)

Some cooks say baking your sweet potatoes before mashing them produces a richer flavor than boiling. I've tried it both ways and can't really tell the difference. If you want to bake them, leave the skins on and put them in the oven at 350 degrees for about 45 minutes. Bake them just until they're tender to a fork. Don't overbake them. You don't want them to get too mushy. If you decide to boil the potatoes instead of baking them, peel them first and boil them until they're tender. Again, don't overcook them. While the sweet potatoes are still hot, mash them together with the butter using a potato masher. In a separate bowl, whisk together the eggs, egg yolks, sugar, nutmeg, salt, bourbon or rye, maple syrup or molasses, vanilla and milk. Gradually stir this mixture in with the mashed sweet potatoes.

Meanwhile, prepare a pie crust from the recipe on Page 41. For a sweet potato pie, partially baking the crust seems to work best. It results in a less soggy crust. Put the pie crust in a pie pan, then place another pie pan, the same size, on top and press down slightly. Bake this for about 8 minutes, reduce heat to 325, remove the top pan and bake for another few minutes until the crust is a light golden brown. Remove your partially baked crust from the oven and let it cool a bit. Then sprinkle the crust with the brown sugar and spoon in the sweet potato filling. (A variation is to spread a thin layer of peanut butter on the crust before filling. Use "natural"-style peanut butter, the kind without sugar or sweeteners.) Bake the pie until the filling is set around the edges but still jiggles ever so slightly in the middle, about 45 minutes. You may have to cover the edges of the crust with foil to prevent them from burning.

Serve with a scoop of vanilla ice cream or fresh whipped cream.

Pecan Pie

1 9-inch pie shell, partially baked
1/3 cup melted butter
1/4 cup dark brown sugar, packed
1/2 cup corn syrup
1/2 cup pure cane syrup
   (or molasses)

4 large eggs, slightly beaten
2 tsps. pure vanilla
1/3 cup heavy cream
1-1/2 to 2 cups whole pecans

Preheat oven to 450 degrees. In a medium mixing bowl, blend melted butter with brown sugar, corn syrup, cane syrup or molasses, eggs, vanilla and cream. Stir together thoroughly. Fold in pecans. Pour into partially baked pie shell (see instructions in previous recipe), turning pecan halves right side up. Place pie pan on a cookie sheet. Bake on bottom rack of oven until just set, around 35 to 45 minutes. Cool completely before serving. Slice with a serrated knife.

Caramel Bourbon Sauce

1 cup sugar
3/4 cup heavy cream

3 tbsps. straight bourbon
1 tsp. fresh lemon juice

In a heavy saucepan cook the sugar over medium low heat, stirring constantly with a whisk, until melted and lightly caramel-colored. Cook, without stirring, swirling pan, until deep golden. Remove pan from heat. Slowly and carefully stir in cream, bourbon and lemon juice. Caramel will start to harden during this process. Return pan to heat and simmer, until the caramel is dissolved. Serve on vanilla ice cream, bread pudding or cream cheese pound cake (recipe below).

Caribbean Cream Cheese Pound Cake

3 sticks butter, softened
8 oz. package regular cream
   cheese, softened
3 cups flour
3 cups sugar

6 eggs and 4 egg yolks
1 tsp. vanilla extract
2 tsps. coconut extract
1 tbsp. lime juice

Preheat oven to 325 degrees. Beat softened butter and cream cheese until smooth. Add 2 eggs, 1 cup flour and 1 cup sugar; beat well. Repeat until all eggs, flour and sugar have been added, beating well after each addition. Add vanilla, coconut extract and lime juice, mixing well. Bake in greased and floured loaf pan for 1 hour, 15 minutes.

Croatian Traditions

"The wonderful flavor of pork fat mingled with sauerkraut and potatoes... Eastern European cooking at its finest."

Turns out I'm a *zec*. Zec is the word Joe Krizman Sr. used to describe outsiders — folks not of Croatian descent. The word sounds like "zetz" and means "rabbit." As in lettuce-eating animal. Salad-eater. By definition, if you are a salad-eater you can't be a Croatian, because Croatians are, as Joe Sr. used to say, "hearty eaters." Meat-and-potatoes people.

Joe Krizman Jr. explains all this to me at a Krizman family dinner. I admit that indeed I am an outsider among these Croatians, being that I'm of English and German extraction. But when I point to the pile of sausage and boiled potatoes on my plate, Joe Jr. concedes that maybe I am not as much of a zec as most zecs.

According to Joe Jr., traditional Croatian cooking doesn't include a lot of veggies. If there's a vegetable on a Croatian's plate, most likely it's cabbage. In the form of sauerkraut or the leaves from whole pickled cabbages, called sauerheads.

Left: Nina Krizman helps her mother, Jenny, make povitica. Above: Sue Krizman, Nina's grandmother.

For three generations, the Krizman family has been making sauerkraut and sauerheads for Kansas City's Eastern European immigrants. But it's sausage, more than sauerkraut, that has earned the family a place in the hearts and bellies of hungry Kansas Citians. From their tiny Strawberry Hill sausage factory and store they have — for more than 60 years — been handcrafting Old World-style bratwurst, knockwurst, kielbasa, blood sausage, barbecue sausage, salami and summer sausage.

Joe Krizman Sr. emigrated to the United States from Croatian Yugoslavia in 1917. Like many Yugoslavian immigrants before and after him, he settled in the Strawberry Hill district of Kansas City, Kan., and was soon working in the meat packing plants in the West Bottoms. In 1921 he married Mary Lacy and eventually had four sons, Dick, Don, Joe Jr. and Bob.

After the fall of the Soviet Union and the end of the Cold War, Eastern European countries that had been under Communist rule began to break up and reestablish old national identities and boundaries. The Republic of Croatia was one of these, splitting from the Yugoslav federation in 1991.

Traditional Croatian cooking is influenced mainly by the traditions of Hungary, Vienna and the Ottoman Turks, who occupied the country between the 15th and 17th centuries.

There are fairly distinct regions within Croatia, each with cooking traditions of its own. Istria is the peninsula in the far northwestern corner of the country. The Dinaric Alps region is the mountainous section of the country along the coast of the Adriatic Sea. Dalmatia is the narrow stretch of land south of the mountains extending to the city of Dubrovnik. The food of these coastal regions has also been influenced by Italian, French and Greek cooking traditions, and includes more fish than does the cooking farther inland.

Croatia's capital, Zagreb, is a culinary region unto itself. Joe Krizman Sr. was born in Lukovdol, a village near the town of Karlovac, which is fairly close to the capital. Zagreb is an ancient city and its food reflects its long history and role in European commerce and cultural development. Zagreb's cuisine is eclectic, sophisticated and more clearly owing to Hungary and Vienna.

In 1939, Joe Sr. and his cousin Matt Grisnik opened a grocery store on Sixth Street, about a half-block north of Elizabeth Street. The gregarious Grisnik was the "up-front man," greeting customers and helping fill orders. But because Joe Krizman was worried about getting caught moonlighting and losing his job at the packing plant, he stayed in the back of the store. There he began making sausage for the store's meat case, and the Krizman family's reputation for making the best wurst was soon established.

Over time, as cost-efficient supermarkets put the squeeze on small grocery stores, and as word of their excellent sausage spread, sausage-making became the family's primary business. These days Krizman's House of Sausage sells most of its products wholesale to many of Kansas City's best restaurants and barbecue joints. But retail customers who care about quality can still buy their sausages direct from the little white meat case in the front of the store.

The House of Sausage is a source of intense family pride even for Krizmans not involved in its daily operations. Garth Krizman is a partner in a Kansas City, Kansas, advertising and graphic design firm. His father is Don, third-born son of Joe Sr. A few years ago Garth designed a logo and product packaging for the family business.

"I'm not there in the back of the store grinding meat and stuffing casings, but the House of Sausage is a part of me," Garth says. "My cousins who work there now are like brothers to me, and I'll always feel like I have a responsibility to the place."

In 1990 Garth married Jenny Regan. She is as Irish as he is Croatian, and is intimately familiar with life in a large extended family with a strong ethnic identity. "Our Regan family get-togethers are a lot like the Krizmans'," Jenny says. "Only we're even louder, and there's even more beer."

Though she's an in-law — an Irish one at that — Jenny Krizman has become the family's designated baker of traditional Croatian pastries.

When it came time to pass the family's Croatian baking knowledge to a younger generation, Garth's grandma Mary chose Jenny to carry the torch.

The first thing Grandma Mary taught Jenny to make was,

Jack Krizman rolls sarma, while his cousin Garth Krizman enjoys a little wine.

Sally Krizman helps herself to some sarma.

technically, not a pastry. It was noodles. Another Croatian tradition. But Jenny says her noodles never measured up to Mary's.

"At most every holiday dinner someone would say, 'These noodles aren't as good as Grandma's,' " Jenny sighs.

But she persisted, and, for her efforts, she was bequeathed Mary's rolling pin, breadboard and cookbooks when Mary passed on.

A few years ago, when they moved to their home in Roeland Park, Kansas, Garth and Jenny were delighted to discover five Croatian women living in a house right across the street. This serendipitous twist of fate gave Jenny an opportunity to put her inherited baking utensils to good use.

The neighbor ladies are sisters and retired, which gives them lots of time to perfect their *povitica*, a Croatian nut bread that has become as much associated with KCK as Strawberry Hill.

When Genevieve, the third-oldest of the sisters, learned of Jenny's interest in traditional Croatian baking, she took Jenny on as an apprentice and began to teaching her the finer points of povitica.

First, Jenny was required to watch Genevieve as she carefully explained each step. The next time, Jenny was allowed to assist

Genevieve as, again, each step was described in detail. Finally, under Genevieve's watchful eye, Jenny tried it herself. Then she tried it again. And then again.

At Christmastime Jenny felt confident enough in her progress that she surprised her Krizman in-laws with povitica for presents.

"They couldn't believe it. They didn't quite know what to expect," Jenny recalls. "But I think I won them over."

As she rolls and stretches dough out on a table covered in a clean white bed sheet, to make povitica for a family dinner the next day, Jenny worries that the edges of the dough are too thick. Genevieve always says thin edges make for a good spiral of filling when the loaf is sliced.

"Krizmans are a tough audience," she laughs, blowing a lock of hair out of her face as she leans over her work, pulling and pinching.

The following day, the Krizman clan gathers at the home of Jack and Barbara Krizman. Jack is a second-generation Krizman American. His father is Bob, second-born son of Joe and Mary. With his uncle Joe Jr. and his cousin Joe III, Jack works at the House of Sausage preserving the family tradition of fine sausages.

"I probably take it for granted," Jack says. "Usually I just think of it as my job. But then someone will say how much they enjoy our sausage, or an older person from the old country will tell us how much our sausage reminds them of home, and then I'm reminded of how what we're doing really is special."

At this dinner the menu is sarma (stuffed cabbage rolls), masnica (a bread with onion and bacon filling), stuffing rolls, cheese strudel, and povitica. Oh yeah… all that and *kiska*, too. Kiska. Which is another name for "Croatian caviar." Which is a euphemism for blood sausage.

When the blood sausage is placed on the table in front of me, I understand that this zec is being tested. Eager to prove myself more than a rabbit — more than some little bunny — I spoon a pile of the kiska on a cracker and jam it in my mouth.

It's actually good. Quite good, in fact. I eat another cracker full. And then a little more. Seeing that I like it, Joe Jr. begins to explain how kiska is made. About that time I realize that I haven't yet talked to Joe Krizman III and I excuse myself.

Joe III and his wife, Mary (that's right, same names as the grandparents), smile as they watch the aunts and uncles and nieces and nephews enjoy the food and the company. "A big part of my growing up was our Sunday dinners at our grandparents' house," Joe says. "The whole family would be jammed into my grandma's tiny little kitchen, all talking at once.

"We don't have as many family dinners as we used to. That makes holidays all the more special."

The younger Krizmans talk about their parents and grandparents with much respect.

Joe Sr. would appreciate that.

By all accounts Joe Sr. was a proud man. He demanded, and earned, the respect of his neighbors, his customers and his family.

"When we sat around the table to eat, all Dad needed to do was clear his throat and we'd all be quiet and pay attention," says Bob, as he pours after dinner shots of slivovitz — plum brandy — for his brothers and guests.

Joe Jr. says his dad was also a man of strong opinions, and he tells a story to make a point. Seems that one day after Joe Jr. had taken over operations of the shop, his father was visiting and became agitated.

"When my dad made sauerheads he would fill the pickle barrels with cabbages and brine and then, to keep the cabbage heads submerged, he would put a big rock on a wooden disk that would push the cabbages down into the brine," Joe Jr. explains. "Well, when I started running things I thought I'd use a five gallon pail filled with water instead of that rock. Seemed a little more sanitary. Well, he saw that pail sittin' on top of the sauerheads and said, 'Now I know why your kraut is slimy. You're not using the rock.' So not only was my problem that I wasn't using a *rock*, I wasn't using *the* rock."

When Joe Jr. tells this story, the entire family listens intently, smiling in anticipation. They've heard this one a hundred times if they've heard it once. They know the punchline by heart. But when Joe delivers it they all laugh as if hearing it for the first time. Stories like this are served up with the same kind of love as are the sarma and the povitica, and serve the same purpose. They affirm, sustain and celebrate the Krizmans' family identity.

Between stories, Don Krizman raises his glass of slivovitz to his daughter-in-law. "Jenny, this is the best povitica I've had in years."

The Krizman clan. That's Grandpa Joe in the framed drawing.

Krizman Family Recipes

and other traditional Croatian dishes

Sarma

Sarma and povitica are probably the two dishes most associated with Croatian culture here in the United States. And the Krizman family excels at making both.
Sarma is thought to have been brought to Croatia by Turkish conquerors in the 15th century.
Here's the Krizman version of this delicious traditional dish.

1-1/2 lbs. ground chuck
1/2 lb. ground pork
1 large whole head pickled
    cabbage ("sauerhead,"
    available at Krizman's House
    of Sausage in Kansas City, Kan.)
3/4 cup uncooked rice
    (not "minute"-style)

1 egg
1 (15 oz.) can tomato sauce
4 cups beef stock or beef broth
2 smoked sausage rings, cut into
    2-inch pieces
12-18 white potatoes, peeled
Salt and pepper to taste

Anna Krizman, youngest daughter of
Garth and Jenny Krizman.

Mix meat, rice and egg together. Season with salt and pepper and set aside. Prepare the cabbage leaves by removing the stem and core from the sauerhead. Remove the outer leaves and rinse with cold water to remove excess brine.

Form egg-shaped meatballs using about 2 tablespoons of the meat mixture. Place one of these meatballs on the thick end of a cabbage leaf and roll it up burrito-style. Secure the sarma (cabbage roll) with a toothpick if necessary. Repeat until all the meatballs are wrapped and rolled.

Make sauerkraut by shredding or chopping the remaining sauerhead.

Cut smoked sausage into 2-inch pieces.

Place half the sauerkraut in the bottom of a large stockpot, roasting pan or electric roasting pan. Place the sarma and sausage pieces on top of the kraut, then top with remaining kraut.

Mix tomato sauce and beef stock with enough water to cover the sarma, sausage and kraut and add this to the pot.

Cover and bring to a boil. Reduce heat and simmer 1-1/2 to 2 hours.

Cut peeled potatoes into quarters and boil under fork-tender. Serve with sarma.

Arlene Krizman, Dick Krizman's wife.

Masnica

This delicious and filling savory bread is a fave at Krizman family events.

1 lb. frozen bread dough, thawed	1 bunch green onions
1 lb. thick-sliced bacon	1 egg, beaten

Let the dough rise. While dough is rising, chop bacon into small 1/2-inch pieces and cook until crisp. Drain well on a paper towel. Wash and dry green onions and chop fine.

Roll dough out into a large rectangle and brush with beaten egg. Sprinkle the bacon and onions over the rolled-out dough. Roll up the dough and place in a well-greased bread pan. Bake at 350 degrees 45 minutes to 1 hour.

Bones

Here's how my friend Garth Krizman describes "bones," a Krizman family eating tradition.

"Seems we always had bones on Monday night. Not sure why, but maybe after a busy first day back at work it was just an easy, cheap meal to make.

"The 'bones' were scraps trimmed off the short end of a rack of spare ribs. Everyone thinks butchers eat the finest cuts of meat. Not so. Butchers eat what they can't sell. Snouts, knuckles, brains — you get the idea. My family ate scraps, 'and liked it!'

"When Grandpa and Uncle Joe trimmed the slabs they saved the last few end ribs and threw them in the freezer. When enough of these 'bones' accumulated a Monday night family meal was convened. Meat for the Masses. The hungry Krizmans gathered to devour the 'unused' meat.

"This attitude toward food is characteristic of our family. If there was a little cole slaw left over at the end of a meal, the bowl was passed around until it was empty.

"As for the actual preparation of the 'bones' they never hickory-smoked the rib ends or anything like that. That would take too much time. They simply boiled 'em for thirty minutes or so, reduced the heat and then dropped in a mess of sauerkraut and a lb. or two of peeled and cut-up potatoes, then simmered it all for about another half hour. No seasoning. If done right — and it's not hard to do it right — the meat just falls off the bone. The wonderful flavor of the pork fat was absorbed by the kraut and potatoes and mmmmm! It was good. We usually used horseradish as a condiment with this meal. And we topped it off with a nice red wine and good heavy bread. Eastern European cooking at its finest and quite typical of a Krizman gathering — which usually consisted of eating, an argument, then hugs goodbye."

Horseradish Sauce

3 tbsps. olive oil
1 medium yellow onion, chopped fine
4 cloves garlic, chopped fine

1/2 cup dry white wine
4-6 tbsps. prepared horseradish
2 cups sour cream

Saute the onion in the olive oil over medium-high heat until the onion begins to caramelize and turn golden brown. Add the garlic and white wine and reduce over medium heat. When the wine is cooked off, remove onion and garlic with slotted spoon and let cool in a medium-sized mixing bowl. When cooled, add the horseradish and sour cream and blend thoroughly. Cover and chill completely. Serve as a condiment with roast beef or pork.

Cheese Strudel

An alternative to making strudel dough is to use store-bought puff pastry sheets.

For the dough:

2-1/2 cups sifted flour
1 egg, beaten
1 teaspoon salt

1/3 cup vegetable oil
2/3 cup very warm water

Mix all ingredients, adding more flour as needed to make a smooth dough that doesn't stick to your hands. Knead until the dough comes off the sides of the bowl. Then knead on a lightly floured work surface until dough is firm. Place the dough in a large bowl or pan, cover with waxed paper and let it rest for about 1 hour.

On a lightly floured work surface roll the dough into a very thin sheet. Preheat oven to 350 degrees.

For the filling:

8 oz. ricotta cheese
8 oz. small-curd cottage cheese
16 oz. large-curd cottage cheese

1 teaspoon salt
1/2 cup sugar
5 egg yolks, beaten stiff

Mix the above ingredients, except the egg yolks, thoroughly. After well mixed, fold in the beaten egg yolks. Spread half the cheese mixture evenly over the rolled-out dough. Roll up the dough jellyroll style and place in a baking pan. Bake at 350 degrees for 30 minutes.

Serve as an appetizer, side dish, or sprinkled with powdered sugar as a dessert.

Apple Strudel

For the dough follow the recipe under Cheese Strudel, above.
An alternative to making strudel dough is to use store-bought puff pastry sheets.

For the filling:

2-3 lbs. Granny Smith
   apples, peeled and
   sliced very thin
2 cups brown sugar

1 teaspoon cinnamon
1/2 lb. finely crushed
   vanilla wafers
2 sticks melted butter

Combine apple slices with sugar and cinnamon. Brush dough with melted butter. Spread crushed vanilla wafers evenly over buttered dough. Then spread apple mixture over the vanilla wafers. Roll jellyroll style. Fold roll into a U-shape and place in a greased shallow baking pan. Bake at 350 degrees for one hour.

Povitica

This wonderful, not-too-sweet dessert is as much a part of Croatian holiday traditions as Christmas Eve Mass.

For the dough:
1/2 cup warm water   2 pkgs. dry yeast
1-1/2 tbsps. sugar

Measure water into bowl. Add sugar and stir. Add yeast and mix until the yeast is dissolved. Let rise until foamy.

1/2 cup milk   1/2 stick unsalted butter
1/2 cup sugar   1/8 cup vegetable oil
1/2 tbsp. salt

Scald milk. Stir in sugar, salt, butter and oil, and cool to lukewarm. Add this to yeast mixture.

2 eggs   5-6 cups flour

Beat eggs and add to yeast/milk mixture. Add half of the flour and mix thoroughly. Gradually add the remaining flour, mixing until dough no longer sticks to fingers or the side of the bowl. Knead on work surface until dough is smooth and elastic. Place in an oiled bowl and let rise until double in volume (1-2 hours).

For the filling:
2-1/2 lbs. English walnuts,   1-1/2 sticks butter
    crushed fine   5 eggs, beaten
3-1/2 cups sugar   2 tbsps. honey
2 cups milk

Boil milk and remove from heat. Add butter to milk and stir until butter is melted. In a large mixing bowl combine crushed walnuts and milk mixture. Mix well. Add sugar, honey, and eggs and mix again.

Spread a clean white sheet (folded to approximately 40 inches x 60 inches) over a table. Flour it well. Turn dough out of bowl onto the middle of the sheet. Place your hands, palms down, on the sheet and push them under the dough. Using the backs of your hands, lift the dough and from the middle of the dough begin to stretch it toward you. Continue to work the dough in this manner until it is paper-thin.

Spread the walnut mixture evenly over the dough. Preheat oven to 350 degrees.

Lift up the edge of the sheet nearest with your hands about as far apart as the width of the dough. Pull the sheet tight and gently shake it until the edge of the dough begins to roll over onto itself. Continue rolling up the dough jellyroll style. Cut the roll into three equal lengths. Fold each of these rolls into a U-shape and place into well-greased pans and let rise for up to an hour.

Brush tops of the povitica with a beaten egg to which a pinch of sugar has been added. Bake at 350 degrees for 1 hour (or slightly longer, depending on the oven). Cool in pan for 15 minutes. Then continue cooling on a rack until completely cooled.

Bob Krizman

The next two recipes aren't traditional Krizman family fare, but are reflective of the kind of food popular in the Zagreb region of Croatia, from which the Krizmans emigrated. I've adapted them to include Krizman sausage.

Stuffed Veal *a la* Krizman

4 veal chops	2 cups breadcrumbs
2 cups grated Guyre or Swiss cheese	1/2 tsp. dried oregano
	1/2 tsp. dried rosemary
8 slices thinly sliced Krizman's salami	1/2 tsp. dried thyme
	1/2 tsp. dried parsley
Olive oil	1 egg, beaten with 1/2 cup milk

Slit a pocket in each chop and insert two slices of salami. Then between the slices of salami stuff about 1/2 cup of grated cheese. Pinch the opening of the chop together as much as possible and use toothpicks to secure. Thoroughly stir the dried herbs into the breadcrumbs. Dip the chops in egg wash, then dredge in breadcrumb mix. Place the breaded chops on a platter and chill for at least 1/2 hour. Cook in olive oil over medium-high heat until golden and crispy on the outside.

For the sauce:

6 tbps. olive oil	1 tbsp. sugar
6 yellow onions, sliced very thin	2 cups dry white wine
4 cloves garlic, minced	2 cups heavy cream

This sauce works best when the onions are sliced so thin they're almost transparent. This requires a very sharp knife and a clean handkerchief to wipe your eyes, as you will definitely shed some tears.

Sauté the sliced onions in the olive oil until golden and beginning to caramelize. Add the white wine and sugar and reduce. When the white wine is reduced by half, add the cream and garlic and reduce again by half.

Serve the veal chops on top of a cup of sauce that has been ladled onto a plate.

Krizman Sausage and Plum Stuffing
for Suckling Pig or Roast Turkey

The Krizmans love stuffing. This stuffing recipe is good with both turkey and suckling pig, both of which are traditional holiday fare in Croatia. Included in this recipe are plums, perhaps the most popular and widely used fruit in Croatia, and sunflower seeds. Sunflowers are an important crop in the former Yugoslavia.

Stuffing:
1 stick butter
1 lb. Krizman breakfast
    sausage
1-1/2 cups prunes, chopped
    for stuffing
2 cups prunes (for cavity)
1 cup sunflower seeds
4 stalks celery, chopped,
    including leaves
1-1/2 cups yellow onion,
    chopped fine

3-4 yellow onions, peeled and
    quartered (for cavity)
1 bunch green onions,
    chopped fine
1/2 cup fresh parsley, choppex
3 cloves fresh garlic, chopped fine
1 (16 oz.) bag bread cubes
    (stuffing mix)
Chicken broth
    (as needed for moisture)
Salt and pepper
1/2 cup maple syrup

Melt the butter in a skillet and stir in the yellow onion and celery. Cook over low heat until the onion is soft, then add sausage (and chopped gizzard, liver and neck meat if cooking turkey). Continue to cook until sausage is thoroughly brown and crumbly. Add the sausage mixture to the bread crumbs, garlic, green onions, parsley, sunflower seeds, and maple syrup. Mix thoroughly with plenty of salt and freshly ground pepper. Spoon into a large casserole and bake in the oven along with the turkey or pig. Baste occasionally with pan juices or with chicken broth and melted butter.

For suckling pig: Preheat the oven to 350 degrees. Rub the pig with the oil and sprinkle with salt and pepper. Fill the cavity with quartered pieces of peeled yellow onion and chopped prunes. Sew the cavity shut. Put the pig on its side on a rack in a shallow roasting pan. Cover the ears and tail with foil so they do not burn. Place in the oven and baste every 20 minutes with melted butter until there are enough pan juices for basting.

Roast about 20 minutes per lb. — 4-1/2 hours for a 15 lb. pig — basting often. Some of the pan juices may be used to baste stuffing as well. Remove foil and cook at least 30 minutes more, until internal temperature is 180 degrees. Remove from oven. Open cavity and discard onions and prunes. Let pig rest at room temperature for 15 minutes before carving.

For turkey (18-20 lbs.): *This recipe requires more than seven hours of cooking time, but most Kansas Citians know that the "low and slow" method produces great results. It is, after all, how barbecue is made.*

Preheat the oven to 350 degrees. Remove the giblets, liver and neck from the body cavity and wash the turkey inside and out with cold water and pat dry with paper towel. Rub the turkey with vegetable oil and sprinkle with salt and pepper. Fill the cavity with quartered pieces of peeled yellow onion and chopped prunes. Cover the cavity with the excess skin at the tail end of the cavity opening. Put the turkey, breast side down, in a large shallow roasting pan. Cover the entire bird with foil. Place in the oven and roast for one hour.

After one hour turn the heat down to 250 degrees and continue roasting for another three hours. Then remove foil, turn the turkey over, breast side up, brush with more vegetable oil, sprinkle with more salt and pepper, cover with foil again and roast for another three hours.

After six hours of roasting at 250 degrees — three breast side down, three breast side up — check the internal temperature of the turkey by inserting a meat thermometer in one of the thighs. If it has not yet reached 170 degrees, return to oven and continue roasting at 250 degrees until the internal temp (measured in the thigh) is 170 degrees.

When internal temp has reached 170, remove turkey from oven and turn oven temp up to 500 degrees. Remove foil, and when oven has reached 500 degrees, return turkey to oven and continue roasting until skin is golden brown, about 10 minutes. Open cavity and discard onions and prunes. Let turkey rest at room temperature for 15 minutes before carving.

Cevapcici

1-1/2 lbs. ground chuck	1 tbsp. chopped fresh dill
1/2 lb. ground lamb	1 tsp. fresh ground pepper
1 tbsp. chopped fresh parsley	1 tbsp. kosher salt
1 tbsp. chopped fresh mint	4 cloves garlic, minced

Put all the ingredients in a large mixing bowl and knead thoroughly, making sure the herbs and spices are completely incorporated. Cover and chill for about 2 hours, then knead again. Shape the meat mixture into small rolls about the length and width of small sausage links. Cook the cevapcici on a grill or under the broiler until cooked through. Serve with sour cream and sliced onions.

The Croatian flag.

The following aren't Krizman family recipes,
but are the kinds of food popular in the Old Country.

Veggie Appetizer
Ajvar

2 large eggplants
3 red bell peppers,
    cored and seeded
3 green bell peppers,
    cored and seeded
2 medium yellow onions,
    halved and sliced thin
3 cloves garlic, chopped fine
4 tbsps. extra virgin olive oil,
    for cooking

2 tsp. sugar
1/2 cup dry white wine
3 tbsps. fresh lemon juice
3/4 cup extra virgin olive oil,
    for dressing
2/3 cup sunflower seeds
2/3 cup fresh parsley, chopped
Salt
Freshly ground pepper

Trim stems from eggplants and cut each in half lengthwise. Salt liberally and place in a colander, skin side down, and let drain for 30 minutes. Cut peppers in quarters lengthwise and lay them flat on a broiling pan skin side up. Rinse eggplant and place on broiling pan skin side up. Broil vegetables until skin is charred, about 12-15 minutes. Remove and place vegetables in a paper bag. Close bag and let veggies rest for about 15 minutes. Remove from bag and peel skins from peppers and eggplant. Cut veggies in about 1-inch pieces.

In a heavy skillet, sauté onion in olive oil over medium-high heat until onions begin to caramelize. Add wine and garlic and let simmer until wine is reduced to about a tablespoon in volume.

In a glass bowl, combine eggplant, peppers, and onion mixture together with olive oil, lemon juice and sunflower seeds. Season with salt and pepper to taste.

Túróscsusza
Noodles with cheese

1 lb. wide egg noodles
8 oz. small-curd cottage cheese
8 oz. ricotta cheese
2 tsp. finely chopped fresh
    or dried dill

1/2 lb. bacon, chopped
    and cooked crisp
1 medium yellow onion,
    chopped fine
2 cloves garlic, minced
4 oz. sour cream

Cook noodles in boiling water. Chop bacon into small pieces, about 1/2-inch long, and cook with chopped onion until crisp. Remove bacon and drain on paper towel, leaving bacon fat in pan. Drain noodles, then stir them and the garlic into the bacon fat. Lower heat and add sour cream. Remove from heat and add the cottage cheese, ricotta cheese and chopped dill. Spoon into a heated dish, sprinkle with the bacon and serve.

Sauerkraut Soup

1 tbsp. olive oil	2 cloves garlic, minced
1 lb. (one ring) Krizman's smoked sausage, sliced into rounds	2-1/2 cups sauerkraut, rinsed
	1 potato cut into 1/2-inch cubes
1-1/2 cups chopped onion	2 tbsp. tomato paste
1 tbsp. paprika	7 cups beef broth
1 cup dry white wine	Salt and pepper

Heat olive oil in a large stock pot over medium heat. Add sausage and onion and cook, stirring often, until onion and sausage begin to caramelize, about 15 minutes. Add paprika, wine and garlic and cook, stirring constantly, for about 2 minutes. Stir in kraut, potato pieces and tomato paste. Add beef broth and stir. Cover pot and bring to a boil. Season with salt and freshly ground pepper. Reduce heat and simmer for about 1-1/2 hours, stirring occasionally.

Serve in soup bowls with crusty bread. Or with *njoki* (recipe follows).

Yugoslavian Dumplings
Njoki

2 lbs. potatoes, peeled and quartered	1 tsp. Hungarian paprika
	1/4 tsp. ground nutmeg
4 whole cloves garlic, peeled	Salt
2 tbsps. butter, melted	Freshly ground pepper
3 egg yolks	2 cups flour
1 cup ricotta cheese	

Boil potatoes and garlic until fork-tender. Drain well and cool just to the point that they can be touched. Process potatoes and garlic with a potato ricer. Using an electric mixer or food processor, blend potato mixture with melted butter, egg yolks, ricotta cheese and seasonings. Gradually add flour and mix until smooth. Roll this dough into long cylinders about 3/4-inch wide. Cut into pieces 1/2-inch thick. Lightly flour dumplings, then place on waxed paper. Dry for about 3 hours. Cook the dumplings in small batches in boiling water. Boil gently until the njoki float to the top. Continue boiling for about a minute. Use a strainer to remove the dumplings. Keep cooked dumplings in a warmed bowl while continuing to cook remaining njoki in small batches.

These dumplings are also excellent as a substitute for the potatoes in the next recipe.

Paprika Potatoes

8-10 medium potatoes, peeled and quartered
2 lbs. Krizman's smoked sausage, sliced into rounds
1 lb. bacon, chopped
1 large onion, chopped fine
1 medium green bell pepper, chopped
1 medium tomato, chopped
4-6 cloves garlic, minced
1/2 tsp. salt
1 heaping tbsp. Hungarian paprika
1 tsp. Vegeta (Croatian seasoning available at gourmet food stores. An alternative is Spice Islands Original Seasoning)
1 cup spaghetti sauce
1 tbsp. sugar
1/4 tsp. freshly ground pepper
1/4 tsp. ground marjoram
Pinch dried basil
2-3 cups water
1 cup Zinfandel red wine

Cook the bacon in a heavy-bottom pan until crisp. Remove bacon and drain on paper towel. Add the onion to the bacon fat and cook until golden. Add the remaining ingredients and stir. Bring to a boil, then reduce heat and simmer until potatoes are tender. Before serving, sprinkle with cooked bacon.

Croatian Potato Salad

8 red potatoes, scrubbed and quartered
1 small onion, chopped
1/4 lb. bacon, chopped
3 tbsps. cider vinegar
2 tbsps. flour
2 tbsps. sugar
1 tsp. salt
1 cup water
2 cloves garlic, minced

Boil potatoes until tender. Remove potatoes and immediately spoon them into a large bowl of ice water. When cooled, drain and place in a large mixing bowl. Cook bacon until crisp. Remove bacon with a slotted spoon and drain on paper towel. Cook chopped onion in bacon fat until it just begins to caramelize. Remove onions with a slotted spoon and add to potatoes. Pour out all but about 2 tbsps. of the bacon fat and reserve. To the remaining bacon fat, gradually add flour, stirring continually until smooth and bubbly. Then gradually stir in the vinegar, sugar, salt and water. Bring to a boil and cook for about 1 minute until sauce is thickened. Add sauce, garlic and bacon to potatoes and onions and stir to coat the potatoes.

Sweet and Sour Potatoes

2 cups cooked ham, cubed
8-10 new red potatoes,
 cooked and cubed
8 dill pickles, diced
1 red onion, quartered,
 then sliced thin

2 Granny Smith apples, cored,
 cut into small chunks
1 cup mayonnaise,
 more or less to taste
1/2 cup sour cream
Salt
Freshly ground pepper

Mix everything above in large glass or stainless steel bowl. Season, cover and chill.

Cabbage and Noodles

1 stick butter
1 large onion, sliced
1 large head cabbage, shredded
4 cloves garlic, minced
1 tsp. salt

1/4 tsp. freshly ground pepper
16 oz. large egg noodles, cooked
 al dente and drained
1 pint sour cream

Melt butter in large stockpot. Add cabbage, onion and garlic and cook over medium heat until it just begins to caramelize. Lower heat. Add salt and pepper and let cook over for another 15-20 minutes. Add noodles and sour cream and stir to blend.

The sons of Joe Krizman: Dick, Bob, Joe Jr., Don.

Jenny and Sue load up their plates.

Pork Chops with Onion Gravy and Sauerkraut

8 thick-cut pork chops

6-8 large onions, chopped

2 tbsps. sugar

Salt and pepper to taste

Preheat oven to 325 degrees. On stovetop, brown chops in a large oven proof skillet over high heat. Add onions, sugar, salt, and pepper. Cover and place in oven and cook for about 1-1/2 to 2 hours.

For the sauerkraut:

2 lbs. Krizman's sauerkraut

1 cup water

1 tbsp. sugar

2 tbsps. butter or bacon fat

2 tbsps. flour

Put sauerkraut, sugar and water in a large stockpot add. Bring to a boil, then lower heat and cook util kraut is soft. In a small saucepan, melt butter or bacon fat. Make a roux by gradually adding flour, continually stirring until smooth and bubbly. Stir this into the kraut. Let simmer on low heat.

For the gravy:

2 cups water (more or less)

2 tbsps. butter or bacon fat

2 tbsps. flour

When the pork chops are done, remove them from skillet. Place skillet back over medium-high heat. To the onions in the skillet, add the butter or bacon fat. When melted, gradually add 2 tbsps. of flour, stirring continually. To this roux and onion mixture, gradually add 2 cups water. Be sure to scrape the caramelized meat and onion bits from the bottom and sides of the skillet.

Serve chops on a bed of sauerkraut with mashed potatoes on the side. Ladle onion gravy over both the chops and potatoes.

Turkish Meat Pies

A popular portable lunch in Croatia

Filo pastry dough (available in the freezer case at most grocery stores)

1 lb. ground chuck

1 medium yellow onion, chopped fine

1 bell pepper, chopped fine

2 cloves garlic, minced

Salt

Pepper

Olive oil

Cook the ground chuck, onions and pepper in olive oil until meat and onions are well browned. Add garlic, salt, and pepper. Place a layer of filo on a greased cookie sheet.

Cover with a thin layer of the meat filling and cover this with another layer of filo that has been brushed with olive oil. Add another thin layer of meat filling and cover with yet another sheet of filo. Repeat until you have five or six layers, with filo on top. Bake at 375 degrees for about 30 minutes, or until filo is golden brown. Cut in 4 inch squares to serve.

Bread Pudding with Plum Brandy Sauce

Slivovitz, a potent plum brandy, is the Croatian national drink. After Krizman family dinners, the men gather in the kitchen and toast one another with shots of slivovitz. Then, after a very few minutes of allowing the men to pretend they still live in a traditional male-dominated society, the women join them for another round of toasting. Secretly the men are relieved. They know it's better this way. Here's a sublime bread pudding that is rendered even more heavenly by a slivovitz sauce.

For the pudding:
3 eggs, beaten
1 cup white sugar
2 -1/2 cups whole milk
1-1/2 tsps. cinnamon
1/2 tsp. nutmeg

12 fresh plums, peeled, pitted and sliced
4 red cooking apples, peeled, cored and sliced
6 cups day-old bread cubes
6 tbsps. butter, cut into pieces

Preheat oven to 350 degrees. In a large bowl, combine eggs, sugar, milk, cinnamon and nutmeg and stir until smooth. Fold in plums, apples and bread cubes until bread is well coated. Pour into buttered 9-by-13 baking dish. Top with pieces of butter. Bake for about 1 hour, until set. Serve warm with slivovitz (plum brandy) sauce.

For the sauce:
1 cup slivovitz
1 lb. butter

2 cups sugar

In a medium saucepan over medium heat, combine slivovitz, butter and sugar. Stir continuously until sugar dissolves and sauce is smooth. Remove from heat and serve hot over warm bread pudding.

Filipino Traditions

*"Cooking is like prayer. You do it with
your heart. Then you give it to others.
And it makes everyone better in their
bodies and souls."*

The Filipino tradition of fiesta is like a state of grace. In this state of grace you are forgiven your reticence to look your neighbor in the eye and know his name and his problems and his hobbies. Your reluctance to reach out or be reached out to is overlooked. And, if the shoe fits, your suburban remoteness and your culturally ingrained ethnocentrism are excused. Your disinclination to try something new is disregarded.

In the Filipino tradition of fiesta, complete strangers are expected, even invited, to come to your house for dinner and to eat off your best china, with your best silverware and to drink your best wine from your best crystal.

In the Philippines fiestas began, centuries ago during Spanish rule, as "feast days" honoring Catholic saints. Over time these holidays evolved into more generalized celebrations of communal faith and community identity. In the towns and villages where fiestas were held, people were expected to offer their homes and hospitality to anyone and everyone who happened by.

Left: Sergio Alaniz with a mouthful of his grandmother Adela Tan's pork barbecue. Above: Nita West.

The history and culture of the Philippines are rich and colorful, like its food.

The country is an archipelago comprising of 7,107 islands. The major islands are Luzon, Mindanao, Palawan, Negros and Samar.

There are more than 65 distinct ethnic and cultural minorities in the Philippines, many of which speak their own languages or dialects.

Beyond the central influence of its indigenous peoples, Filipino culture reflects the strong influence of the nations that have conquered, colonized and conducted commerce with the country over the last two millennia. Chinese merchants were probably among the first outsiders to travel to the islands that eventually became the Philippines, and their influence has remained. It is clearly evident in Filipino food. Eggrolls, soy sauce, fish sauce, the specific use of certain vegetables, as well as cooking techniques such as stir fry, are examples of culinary customs left behind by the Chinese.

Another important historic and cultural influence on the development of the Philippines was India. This is reflected in the dominant native language, which contains many words with Sanskrit origins and in the older, Hindu-influenced religious practices of many indigenous groups.

In 1565, Spain began colonizing the Philippines. Spain's control of the islands lasted for 333 years, and the influence of Spanish culture in the Philippines is pervasive, most obviously in that more than 75 percent of Filipinos are Roman Catholic. In fact, the nation is named after Spain's King Philip. Filipino foods such as empanadas are a legacy of Spanish rule.

The Philippines were an American colony for nearly 50 years, beginning in 1898 and American influence remains strong to the present. English is one of the country's two official languages. Unfortunately, American fast-food culture has taken root in the Philippines, the homogenizing effect of which is seen most in larger cities.

Jose Bayani says that Filipinos are a very resilient people, in part because of foreign domination for much of their modern history. "We are very religious, mostly very Christian," he says. "But we are also quite fatalistic. We tend to believe in fate and that things will be what they will be. We have a saying 'Bahala na!' which is like the French saying 'Que sera sera,' or the American expression 'Whatever!' "

Jose Bayani, president of the Filipino Association of Greater Kansas City, explains it all this way: "Fiestas are for everybody. Nobody is excluded. There is dancing, singing, there are parades and , of course, lots of eating. Everyone in town is expected to provide food for their neighbors, whether you know them or not. And you are expected to go out and about to other homes to accept the hospitality of other families. And not just families you already know. In fact, it's almost better if you don't know the family in the house you are visiting. Because it gives you the opportunity to get to know somebody new, and by the time you've eaten their food and sat in their chairs you've made a friend."

This pretty much describes my experience at the home of Adela and Michael Tan. I am, in fact, a complete stranger when I cross the threshold into their house. But I as I eat their food and sit in their chairs and I make new friends.

About 30 new friends.

Almost an entire choir of new friends. A good portion of the alto and soprano sections of the Sampaguita Choral Group show up for dinner at the Tan's the evening I am there, along with a few basses and tenors.

And while the singing is wonderful, the food is sublime.

꙲꙲꙲꙲ ❀ ꙲꙲꙲꙲

Another Filipino tradition is to lay an entire meal right out on the table, rather than serve the dishes one at a time. In that spirit, the Filipinos with whom I am dining at Adela Tan's house lay it all right out for me. All at once, all of Adela's friends begin to tell me about the Filipino food of which I am about to partake.

"This is chicken adobo. It's one of our national dishes."

"These are lumpia. They're basically eggrolls."

"Here. Try this. It's a vinegar garlic hot sauce. Very Filipino."

"That's a shrimp sauce. Very strong. To be honest, it's an acquired taste."

"Isn't that chutney pretty? It's made with tomatoes and mangos."

It is all lovely. The food and the friendly, informed descriptions of it offered for my benefit.

Yet another tradition is to use banana leaves, shiny and bright green, as part of the presentation of the meal. Each of the dishes Adela places on the table is set on its own banana leaf. This accentuates the Asian and tropical

origins of the food, making the experience that much more exotic for me.

It is at this dinner that I feel, at first, most like an outsider, that the culture I am experiencing is least like my own. But, perhaps because they sense this, or, more likely, because it is their nature to do so, it is at this dinner that my hosts work hardest to make me feel welcome.

As I begin to acquaint myself with a few of my many dinner companions and to sample the colorful and fragrant dishes lovingly arranged on Adela's dining room table, I notice a girl of about 8 approach one of the adults. The adult reaches affectionately for the child, at which point the girl takes the hand extended to her and touches it to her own forehead. Then she scampers off to the kitchen.

"What was that I just saw?" I ask Alcy Malkmus, one of Adela Tan's choirmates who has been explaining to me about adobo.

"By touching the adult's hand to her forehead she was receiving a blessing," says Alcy. "It's customary and a courtesy that children up to a certain age seek the blessing of their adult hosts when they come visiting."

Rolando Salvatierra and Michael Tan.

Adela Tan finds great joy in cooking for her friends and family.

✖✖✖✖ ❁ ✖✖✖✖

Adobo is a Filipino cooking technique that uses lots of vinegar in the preparation of fish or meat. This has two benefits. The fish and meat are infused with a strong, rich flavor and the food is naturally protected, to a degree, against spoilage. In poorer rural areas of the Philippines where refrigeration is sometimes rare, this can be particularly advantageous.

Adela Tan's chicken adobo renders meaningless the old cliché "tastes like chicken." Nothing else tastes like this. It's a chorus of flavors, with deep, bass tones of soy sauce and garlic and bright soprano notes of vinegar and bay leaf. For a plain folk dish it is delightfully complex.

Adela doesn't cook professionally. But she does cook passionately.

I ask Adela about the importance of food in Filipino culture.

"Of course, in the Philippines, this food isn't unusual," she says. "It's just the way we eat. But here in the States, it takes on greater significance. For Filipinos living here in America this food is a way of expressing our identity. It's a way of connecting with our home and with each other."

Jose Bayani, who is not only the president of the Filipino Association but also the founder and director of the Sampaguita Choral Group, chimes in. "Food plays the same role in Filipino culture as it does in other cultures. It's a binding agent. It brings and keeps people together. But perhaps because the Philippines are still a developing country and tradition still plays an important part in everyday life there, traditional foods are more important there than in American culture."

I nod thoughtfully as I consider Jose's and Adela's theories. I take a bite of the lumpia on my plate. And then it occurs to me that maybe the real reason food is so important in Filipino culture is that Filipino food just tastes so darn good.

I share this thought with Jose and Adela.

"I cannot disagree," says Jose.

✖✖✖✖ ❁ ✖✖✖✖

"For me the cooking is maybe as important as the food," says Adela Tan. "Cooking is like prayer. You do it with your heart. Then you give it to others. And it makes everyone better in their bodies and souls."

I look around the room at the bodies and souls who have been made better by the prayer of Adela's cooking.

I am happy to count myself among them.

"So," I say. "I've been hearing all night long about this choir of yours. You all going to sing a few numbers, or what?"

In unison the response is, "We thought you'd never ask!"

Jose takes his position at Adela's upright piano and after a few tune-up chords and some clearing of throats, the singing begins.

The first four songs are sung in Tagalog, the primary language of the Philippines. I recognize not a single word but cannot stop smiling even so. Perhaps I am mirroring the smiles of the singers. They are performing their songs with gusto. I am only a few feet away, yet they are projecting as if to the last row of a large concert hall. I can only conclude that though I asked them to sing, I am not their audience. They are singing for themselves. Like their food, this is an expression of their identity.

After the selection of Filipino folk songs, the group takes requests. A few of the guests ask for a Broadway tune and soon we are serenaded with "Try to Remember" from "The Fantasticks" and "Somewhere" from "West Side Story."

Jose Bayani laughs as his choir members put away their music and return to the dining room for some more food and conversation. "Filipinos just love to sing," he says. "In fact the karaoke industry is kept alive almost entirely by Filipinos."

⚒⚒⚒ ✿ ⚒⚒⚒

And so there has been singing and eating and the welcoming of strangers. It's been something of a fiesta.

At the end of a fiesta, as Filipino villagers prepare to return to their own homes from their night of visiting and eating, a host may present her guest with a "BH." BH stands for "bring home" and it may be a brown bag or a foil wrapped dish in which the host has put some of the food that she noticed her guest especially enjoyed.

For my BH, Adela Tan wrapped up an experience I shall never forget. Though, according to tradition, I am too old to touch the hand of my host to my forehead, the hospitality I have been shown touched my heart. And I have received the blessing.

Jose "Ping" Bayani, Katie Lansangan, P.J. Alaniz, Cassie Sundberg, Ned Rabang and Letty Rabang.

❈❈❈ ✿ ❈❈❈

Tan Family Recipes
and other traditional Filipino dishes

❈❈❈ ✿ ❈❈❈

Chicken Adobo

*This is one of the national dishes of the Philippines. It is warm and intense —
like the Filipino people. (Pork and beef may be substituted for chicken.)*

5 lbs. chicken pieces
1 cup white vinegar
1 cup light soy sauce
1 tbsp. salt
1 tbsp. black pepper
1 bay leaf

10-12 cloves garlic, chopped fine
1 medium yellow onion,
   chopped fine
6 cloves garlic, chopped fine
2 tbsps. vegetable oil

Rinse chicken under cold water and pat dry with paper towel. Put meat and all other ingredients, except garlic and oil, into a heavy saucepan. Bring to boil over high heat.

Boil uncovered for about 3 minutes. Cover, reduce heat and let simmer for 30-40 minutes or until the meat is tender but not falling off the bone.

Remove chicken from pan. Bring liquid back to a boil, then simmer until sauce is thickened. Set aside.

In a heavy skillet, sauté six cloves garlic in vegetable oil until golden brown. Add cooked meat and cook for 2 minutes in high heat. Add the thickened sauce. Serve with white boiled rice.

Ping and Adela.

Gingered Fish in Sweet and Sour Sauce
Escabeche

2-3 lbs. white fish, whole
1-1/2 cups vegetable oil
1 tbsp. shredded gingerroot
3-4 cloves garlic, chopped fine
1 medium yellow onion, sliced
1 medium carrot, sliced
1 medium green bell pepper, diced

1/2 cup vinegar
3 tbsps. brown sugar
1 tsp. salt
1 tbsp. cornstarch
1 cup water
2 tbsps. *patis* (fish sauce)

Clean fish keeping the heads and tails intact. Cut the body crosswise. Pat dry with paper towel. Rub fish with salt. Fry in vegetable oil until crispy and golden brown. Set fish aside.

In a medium mixing bowl, add vinegar, sugar, patis, cornstarch and water. Blend well.

In a clean heavy skillet, heat about 3 tablespoons vegetable oil. Sauté garlic until golden brown, then add ginger, onions, carrots and green pepper. Stir frequently. Add cornstarch mixture and bring to boil; stir until sauce thickens. Season with salt and/or patis to taste. Add fish and let simmer in the sauce over high heat for about a minute.

Transfer the fish to a serving platter. Pour the sauce over the fish and arrange vegetables around the platter's edge.

Sarciado

2-3 lbs. white fish, whole
2 cups vegetable or peanut oil
3 cloves garlic, chopped fine
1 medium yellow onion,
    chopped fine
2 medium ripe tomatoes, sliced
1/2 cup green onions, chopped

1/2 cup *kinchai* (Chinese celery),
    chopped
2 tbsps. *patis* (fish sauce)
1 cup water or fish stock
2 eggs, beaten
Salt

Clean and scale fish keeping the head and tail intact. With a sharp knife, make cross hatch cuts on both sides of the body of the fish. Rub fish with salt. Heat one cup of oil in heavy skillet and fry the fish until crisp and brown on both sides. Remove fish and set aside. Discard oil. In a clean skillet heat a couple tablespoons of oil. Sauté the garlic until golden brown. Add yellow onions and cook until soft and transparent. Add sliced tomatoes, green onions, kinchai and patis. Cook until tomato is soft and pulpy. Add water (or stock) and cook for about five minutes, until sauce thickens. Pour in the beaten eggs and gently stir into the sauce. Cook for until the eggs are cooked soft and no longer runny. Pour sauce onto serving platter and place fish on top to serve.

Pancit Malabon

8 oz. package rice noodles
1 tsp. annatto powder (*atchuete*)
1 cup chicken broth
2 tbsps. patis (fish sauce)
1 tbsp. lemon juice
1/2 lb. shrimp, shelled and
    de-veined
1 cup finely crushed *chicharon*
    (fried or sun-dried pork rinds)

1 clove garlic, chopped fine
2 tbsps. vegetable oil
2 green onions, chopped fine
Hard boiled egg slices
Lemon wedges
Salt

Boil noodles for 20 minutes or until just tender. Drain well and set aside. Sauté garlic and shrimp in vegetable oil. Stir in chicken broth and annatto powder. Season with salt to taste. Set aside.

In a small mixing bowl, stir together lemon juice and fish sauce. In a large mixing bowl, toss the noodles with the fish sauce mixture. Stir in the chicharon. Add chicken broth and shrimp. Mix well to coat all pieces.

Place the noodles on a serving platter. Pour the chicken and shrimp mixture on top of the noodles. Arrange egg slices on top and arranges lemon wedges around the edges. Sprinkle with green onions.

Oxtail Stew
Kare-kare

4-5 lbs. oxtail and/or beef shank
8 cups water
1 tsp. salt
2 tbsps. *patis* (fish sauce)
3 tbsps. vegetable oil
2 tbsps. annatto (*atchuete*) oil
   or powder
2 medium yellow onions,
   chopped fine
6 cloves garlic, chopped fine

1/2 cup rice, browned and
   powdered (see below)
1/2 cup peanut butter
1 lb. fresh string beans
1 large eggplant
1 lb. *pechay* (bok choy)
1 tbsp. *kinchai* leaves (Chinese
   celery), chopped fine
1 banana heart
Bagoong or shrimp sauce

Clean oxtail and cut into 3-inches pieces. Slice beef shank in 1/2-inch-thick pieces. Put oxtail and beef shank in pressure cooker with just enough water to cover. Add salt. Cook for 1 hour. (If pressure cooker is not an option, simmer meat in a covered stockpot until tender.) Meat should be tender but not falling off the bone.

For powdered rice: Toast uncooked rice in a heavy skillet over medium heat, stirring frequently to obtain an even golden brown color. Process rice in a blender until rice is reduced to flour-like powder.

In a small saucepan, dissolve peanut butter in one cup broth from pressure cooker (or stockpot).

Wash all vegetables. Trim and cut string beans into 1-inch pieces. Cut eggplant lengthwise into wedges. Separate pechay into single leaves. Slice banana heart crosswise.

Sauté garlic and onion until onion is soft. Add annatto oil or powder. Add meat pieces, leaving liquid in pressure cooker (or stockpot). Cook over high heat, stirring frequently. Season with patis.

Remove fat from the broth in the pressure cooker (or stockpot), then stir in peanut butter mixture and powdered rice, stirring frequently while bringing to boil. Add vegetables and bring to a boil. Cook for about 10 minutes or until the vegetables are tender but still intact. Season with salt or patis. Garnish with celery leaves. Serve with *bagoong*.

Adela, Samantha and Michael Tan.

Eggrolls
Lumpia

1 pkg. eggroll wrappers
1 cooked chicken breast, diced
1/2 lb. ground pork, cooked
1/2 lb. cooked shrimp
4-6 cloves garlic, chopped fine
1 medium yellow onion, chopped fine
2 cups shredded cabbage
1 cup green beans, sliced thin julienne-style
1 cup celery, chopped fine

1 bunch green onions, chopped fine
2 tbsps. cooking oil
1 tbsp. *patis* (fish sauce)
2 tsps. salt
2 tbsps. light soy sauce
1/2 tsp. black pepper
1 egg, beaten (for sealing wrappers)
Vegetable oil for frying

In a heavy skillet, sauté garlic and yellow and green onions until onions are soft and transparent. Add cooked chicken, pork and shrimp and fry over high heat for 2 to 3 minutes. Add the beans, celery and cabbage and cook until vegetables are just tender. Add patis, salt, pepper and soy sauce. Reduce heat and cook for another two or three minutes over medium heat. Drain and cool this mixture in a colander.

Place an eggroll wrapper on work surface and put about 1 tablespoon of the meat/vegetable mixture in the middle of the wrapper. Fold one corner of the wrapper over the filling. Repeat this step with two more corners. At this point, your eggroll should look a bit like an unsealed envelope. Roll the filled and covered part of the eggroll toward and over the remaining corner of the wrapper. Use some of the beaten egg to seal the edges of the wrapper. Repeat this process until all the filling is used.

Fill a heavy skillet or pot with enough oil to cover the eggrolls. Heat the oil to 365 degrees. In small batches, cook the eggrolls until crispy and golden brown on both sides. Drain on paper towel. Serve with a sweet and sour sauce or a vinegar and garlic sauce

(Recipes on the following page.)

Vinegar and Garlic Sauce

1 cup rice (or cider) vinegar	1/8 tsp. salt
4-5 cloves garlic, crushed	1 tsp. red pepper flakes

Mix all ingredients together. To allow flavors to blend well, store in an airtight container and let sit for a few hours before serving.

Sweet and Sour Sauce

1/4 cup rice vinegar	2-3 drops hot pepper sauce
1/4 cup sugar	2 tbsps. catsup
1/4 teaspoon salt	2 tsps. cornstarch
1/2 cup water	1 tbsp. water

In a small pan combine vinegar, sugar, salt, water, pepper sauce and catsup. Boil for two minutes. In a small bowl combine water and cornstarch. Stir well to blend and then stir into sauce. Cook for 3 more minutes at medium heat.

Little Meat Pies
Empanaditas

For the pastry:
1 (14 oz.) package double-crust pastry (makes about 12 to 16 4-inch squares); you can also use wonton wrappers

For the filling:

1 tbsp. vegetable or corn oil	1/2 lb. ground veal
3 cloves garlic, chopped fine	1/2 lb. ground pork
1/2 small yellow onion, chopped fine	1 cup ground or chopped chicken
	Salt
1 small ripe tomato, seeded and diced	Freshly ground pepper

Roll pastry to a thickness of 1/8 inch. Cut into 4-inch squares. (If you are using wonton wrappers, you don't have to do this. They're already cut for you.). Set aside.

In a medium skillet, heat oil. Saute garlic, onion and tomatoes. Cook until garlic is brown and onions turn transparent. Add veal, pork and chicken. Season with salt and pepper. Cook for 20 to 25 minutes, until meat is done. Cook for 5 minutes longer. Allow mixture to cool.

Preheat oven to 400 degrees. Put about a tablespoonful of filling in the center of each square. Fold to form a triangle. Wet edges with water and seal. Arrange on a cookie sheet and bake for 25 to 30 minutes.

Wrapped Plantains
Turon

6 ripe plantain bananas (If plantains are not available, regular bananas may be substituted.)

1 package eggroll wrappers

1 cup drained, shredded jackfruit

3 cups brown sugar

2 cups vegetable oil

1 tsp. vanilla extract

1 egg, beaten

Peel then cut each banana into four equal pieces. In a medium mixing bowl, thoroughly combine brown sugar and vanilla. Roll individual banana pieces in brown sugar mixture and set aside. Place an eggroll wrapper on work surface and place one piece of the banana and two strips of shredded jackfruit in the middle of the wrapper. Fold one corner of the wrapper over the filling. Repeat this step with two more corners. At this point, your roll should look like an unsealed envelope. Roll the filled and covered part of the eggroll toward and over the remaining corner of the wrapper. Use some of the beaten egg to seal the edges of the wrapper. Set aside until all fruit is used. Fill a heavy skillet or pot with enough oil to cover the wrapped bananas. Heat the oil to 365 degrees. In small batches, cook the wrapped bananas until crispy and golden brown on both sides. Drain on paper towel. Dust with powdered sugar. Best when served warm.

Cantaloupe Cooler

1 cantaloupe, halved and seeded

1 cup (or more) sugar

Water

In a food processor puree the pulp and juice from the cantaloupe. Add sugar and puree for another minute or so. Add a few cups of cold water and puree a bit more. Pour this mix into a large pitcher and add more water (and sugar, if desired) until the desired consistency and sweetness is desired. The ideal consistency is actually quite watery. And if pretty little bits of pulp are floating in the drink, so much the better. Chill before serving, or add lots of ice. *Nothing better on a hot and humid summer day!*

꙰꙰ ❁ ꙰꙰

The following are not Tan family recipes, but do reflect Filipino folk cooking traditions.

Catfish Sinigang

Sinigang can be made with fish, pork, chicken or beef.
Most commonly it is made with a freshwater fish.

1/2 cup or more lemon or lime
    juice (to taste)
    (or 1 cup or more green
    tamarind, crushed and cut
    into two or three pieces)
5 cups rice water, the water left
    over from washing your rice
1 cup finely sliced onion
1/4 cup fresh ginger, julienned
2 cups sliced tomato

1 large or two small daikon
    (Chinese radish), peeled and
    sliced thin, diagonally
2 lbs. catfish filets
2 tbsps *patis* (fish sauce)
2 bunches of greens, cleaned and
    stemmed (mustard, collard,
    turnip or spinach)
Chopped scallions for garnish

If you would rather not have the chipped shells and seeds of tamarind in the final product, tie the tamarind loosely in a piece of cheesecloth, which you can remove later. Simmer water, lemon or lime juice or tamarind, onion, ginger and tomato lightly for one-half hour. Add water if it appears to cook away too quickly.

Add daikon and simmer 10 more minutes. Add fish and cook for another 5 to 10 minutes, until the fish is cooked through. Remove tamarind bundle at this point and add patis.

Add greens and cook just until soft. Garnish with chopped scallions. Serve with rice and a small bowl of the broth.

Coconut Chicken

2 lbs. chicken pieces
4 cloves garlic, chopped fine
3 tbsps. peanut oil
1/2 yellow onion, chopped fine
2 tbsps. patis

1/4 tsp. pepper
1 cup sweetened, shredded
    coconut
3 cups chicken stock
1/4 cup chopped green onions

Preheat oven to 350 degrees. In a large mixing bowl toss garlic, onion, chicken pieces, patis, coconut and pepper. Place in a baking dish with 1 cup stock. Cover and bake for 1 hour. Uncover. Turn oven to broil setting and brown chicken under broiler. Sprinkle with scallions and serve over white rice or with rice noodles.

Rubbed and Grilled Steak with Pineapple Rice

For Kansas Citians, who, as a population, are more skilled in the smoking and grilling arts than those of most other cities, this recipe should be both a snap and a delight.

For the steak:

2 lbs. sirloin steak	1 tsp. chili powder
1-1/2 tbsps. seasoned salt	2 cloves garlic, chopped fine
2 tbsps. brown sugar	Freshly ground pepper

Combine salt, sugar, garlic, chili powder and pepper. Rub seasoning on both sides of meat and wrap tightly in plastic wrap and chill in refrigerator overnight.

The next day, remove the steak from the refrigerator about an hour before cooking. Prepare a fire in a kettle grill such as a Weber. Use natural lump charcoal for your fire and do not use lighter fluid. Before putting the steaks on the grill, soak a few chunks of apple wood in water or apple juice for about 30 minutes. When your fire is good and hot and the coals are nice and gray with ash, place the wood chunks on the fire and start your grilling. If you like grill marks on your meat, let the grill rack get hot before putting your steak on it. Grill the steak over a fire to medium well.

2 cups white rice	1 medium yellow onion,
2 cups beef stock	chopped fine
1 cup unsweetened coconut milk	3 cloves garlic, chopped fine
1 cup unsweetened pineapple	Butter
juice	Salt
	Freshly ground pepper

In a heavy saucepan, saute onion and garlic in butter over medium heat until onions just begin to caramelize. Add rice and stir to coat. Season with salt and pepper. Add stock, coconut milk and pineapple juice. Bring to a boil. Cover, reduce heat and cook until rice is tender and fluffy, about 20 minutes.

To serve: Chop steak into cubes and serve over hot rice. Garnish with pieces of canned or fresh pineapple.

Adela and her friend Nita West prepare to serve the adobo.

Hot and Sour Shrimp with Spinach and Cashews

1 lb. large shrimp, uncooked, peeled, de-veined
1/2 cup plus 2 tbsps. dry sherry
1 tbsp. fresh ginger, peeled and grated
1/2 cup chicken stock
2 tbsps. soy sauce
2 tbsps. catsup
1 tbsp. cornstarch
1 tbsp. rice vinegar (white wine vinegar may be substituted)
1 tbsp. sugar
1 tsp. sesame seed oil
1/4 tsp. cayenne pepper
6 tbsps. peanut oil
1/2 cup cashew halves
1 bunch fresh spinach, washed and trimmed
1 red bell pepper, diced
1 green bell pepper, diced
3 cloves garlic, chopped fine
1 bunch green onions, cut diagonally in 1-inch pieces

Combine shrimp, sherry and grated ginger in large bowl. Cover and refrigerate for 30 minutes. Mix remaining 2 tablespoons sherry, chicken stock, soy sauce, ketchup, cornstarch, rice vinegar, sugar, sesame oil and cayenne pepper in small bowl. Heat 2 teaspoons peanut oil in wok or heavy large skillet over high heat. Add cashews and stir-fry for 1 minute. Transfer cashews to plate using slotted spoon. Add spinach to skillet and stir-fry until just wilted, about 1 minute. Divide spinach among plates. Add 2 teaspoons peanut oil, bell peppers and garlic to skillet and stir-fry for 1 minute. Add remaining 2 teaspoons peanut oil, shrimp mixture and onions and stir- fry for 1 minute. Stir stock mixture, add to skillet and cook sauce until clear and thick, stirring frequently, 2 minutes. Spoon sauce and shrimp over spinach. Sprinkle with extra cashews and serve.

Luzon Rice

3 tbsps. peanut oil
4 cloves garlic, chopped fine
1 small yellow onion, chopped fine
3 lbs. chicken, cut in pieces
1 cup ham, cubed
1 stick pepperoni, sliced thin
1/2 lb. pork loin or boneless pork chop, boiled for 15 minutes, then cut into 1/2-inch cubes
2 cups uncooked rice (glutinous rice preferred)
2 (12 oz.) cans coconut milk
1/2 cup chicken stock
1 bay leaf
1/8 tsp. paprika
3 large shrimp, peeled and de-veined
Salt to taste
1 cup frozen peas, thawed and drained
Hard-boiled eggs, sliced

In a stockpot, sauté garlic and onion until onion is soft and translucent. Add chicken, shrimp, pork, ham and pepperoni and cook for another 3-4 minutes. Add rice and stir to coat. Add coconut milk, chicken stock, bay leaf, salt and paprika. Bring to a boil. Reduce heat, cover and let simmer until rice is tender, about 20-30 minutes. Stir in peas. Garnish with hard-boiled eggs.

Beef Adobo in Coconut Milk
Adobong Baka sa Gata

3 lbs. stewing beef, cubed	1 tbsp. freshly ground pepper
3/4 cup rice or cider vinegar	1 tbsp. sugar
8 cloves garlic, chopped fine	4 tbsps. peanut oil
1/2 cup soy sauce	1/2 yellow onion, chopped fine
4 bay leaves	1 (12 oz.) can coconut milk
1-1/2 tbsps. peppercorns	1 tbsp. *patis* (fish sauce)

In a large stockpot add beef, vinegar, garlic, soy sauce, bay leaves, peppercorns, ground pepper and sugar. Stir to thoroughly coat meat and let marinate in the refrigerator for a couple of hours. Bring to stove and bring to a boil. Reduce heat and let simmer for an hour or until beef is tender. Add a bit of coconut milk if necessary to keep mixture moist while cooking.

In a heavy skillet sauté onion in oil until caramelized. Add beef from vinegar sauce mixture and cook until well browned. Stir in patis, coconut milk and the vinegar sauce. Simmer for 5 minutes, stirring constantly.

Pork Puchero

2 lbs. Boston butt, cubed	1 bunch bok choy, chopped, leaves included
1 lb. chorizo, cut in 1/2-inch pieces	1 can water chestnuts, drained
1 bunch green onions, chopped, white parts included	1 lb. fresh green beans, trimmed
3 stalks celery, chopped, leaves included	1 bell pepper (green, red, yellow or orange), diced
	6 cloves garlic, chopped fine

In a large stockpot cover pork with water and bring to a boil. Reduce heat and let simmer for a couple of hours until pork is very tender. Remove pork from the pot and set aside. Add green beans and bok choy to pot and continue simmering.

In a heavy skillet, sauté celery, bell pepper, green onions, garlic and chorizo in oil, until chorizo is cooked through. Add water chestnuts and cook a few minutes longer. Add the vegetables from the pot and the pork and stir together over medium-high heat. Serve over rice.

Crispin Lansangan contemplates his next move.

Grilled Eggplant Salad

8 Chinese eggplants	8 tsps. peanut oil
Kosher salt	Salt
8 cloves garlic, crushed	Freshly ground pepper
8 tsps. rice or cider vinegar	Fresh cilantro

Trim stems from eggplant and slice lengthwise. Salt each slice generously with kosher salt and let drain in a colander or on paper towels for 30 minutes.

Prepare a fire in a kettle-type grill, such as a Weber. Use natural lump charcoal for your fire and do not use lighter fluid. Before putting the eggplant on the grill, soak a few chunks of apple wood in water or apple juice for about 30 minutes. When your fire is good and hot and the coals are nice and gray with ash, place the wood chunks on the fire and start your grilling.

You may want to make this salad when you are grilling chicken, steaks or pork chops.

Rinse eggplant slices. Pat dry with paper towel. Lay each slice of eggplant on the grill skin side up. Grill until eggplant is tender and the flesh side is golden brown. Grill on skin side until skin just begins to blacken. Remove from grill.

Cut grilled eggplant into 1-inch pieces. Toss eggplant pieces with crushed garlic, vinegar and peanut oil. Season with salt and pepper. Garnish with cilantro leaves.

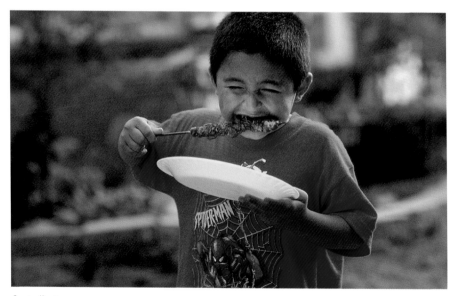

Sergio Alaniz.

Garlic Spinach in Coconut Milk

3 bunches fresh spinach, washed
    and trimmed
2 tbsps. butter
1 small yellow onion, chopped fine
8 cloves garlic, sliced very thin
2 tsps. cumin seeds
1-1/2 tsps. mustard seeds
1 (12 oz.) can coconut milk
4 whole cloves
3 tsps. turmeric

1-1/2 tsps. chili powder
1/4 cup fresh ginger, grated
1/4 cup fresh lime juice
1 tbsp. cilantro, chopped
2 tbsps. fresh mint, chopped
2 ripe tomatoes, peeled, seeded
    and chopped
Freshly ground pepper
Salt

In a large heavy skillet or stockpot, saute the onions and garlic in the butter until the onions are soft and translucent. Add the cumin seeds and mustard seeds and cook for a few more minutes. Add spinach and cook until just wilted. Remove spinach to a serving platter and set aside.

Pour the coconut milk into the skillet, then add the cloves, turmeric, chili powder, ginger, lime juice, cilantro and mint. Bring to a boil, reduce heat and let simmer for about 5 minutes. Remove cloves. Pour coconut milk sauce onto spinach. Season with salt and pepper to taste. Garnish with chopped tomatoes.

Meatballs and Noodles
Sotanghon Bola-Bola

1 lb. ground pork
1 cup breadcrumbs
1/2 yellow onion, chopped fine
2 eggs, beaten
1 tbsp. salt
1/4 tsp. pepper
4 tbsps. peanut oil

6 cloves garlic, chopped fine
1/2 yellow onion, sliced very thin
4 cups chicken or ham stock
1-1/2 pounds sotanghon or bean
    noodles, soaked in 1 cup water
2 tbsps. soy sauce
4 green onions, chopped fine

Combine pork, breadcrumbs, onion, egg, salt and pepper and form into balls about 1 inch in diameter. Saute garlic in peanut oil until just beginning to brown. Add stock and bring to a boil. Add meatballs, bring back to a boil, reduce heat and simmer until meatballs are cooked through. Add the noodles and cook for another 10 minutes or so. Season with soy sauce and pepper. Sprinkle with green onions and serve.

Egg Balls
Yema

4 cups milk	I teaspoon vanilla extract
3/4 cup sugar	2 cups confectioner's sugar
10 egg yolks	

In a saucepan, simmer milk over low heat until it is reduced to 1 cup. Add sugar and stir until well blended. Remove from heat. Let cool. Stir three tablespoons of the sweetened milk into the egg yolks. Gradually, stir the yolks into the milk. Stir in vanilla. Return to stove. Over low heat, stir until mixture thickens. Remove from heat and let cool. When cooled, make balls from the mixture. Each ball should use about 1 tablespoon of the mixture. Roll balls in confectioner's sugar before serving.

Halo-Halo

4 cups water	1/4 cup tapioca
I cup diced sweet potatoes	(quick-cooking type)
I cup sweet rice powder	1/2 cup sugar
(available at Asian groceries)	3 tablespoons water
1-1/2 cups coconut milk	I cup jackfruit
(available at Asian groceries)	(available at Asian groceries),
I cup diced plantains	cut into strips

In a saucepan, bring water and coconut milk to a boil. Add 1/4 cup sugar, reduce heat and simmer. Add sweet potatoes and plantains and continue simmering until sweet potatoes are about half cooked. Add 3 tablespoons water to sweet rice powder. From the rice powder mixture, form little balls, about the size of marbles. Drop balls into the coconut milk/sweet potato mixture. Add tapioca, the remaining sugar and jackfruit. Stir and cook until sweet potatoes are tender. May be served hot or cold.

Chocolate Rice Pudding
Champorado

I cup sweet sticky rice	1/2 cup unsweetened cocoa
(available at Asian groceries)	(or more to taste)
2-1/2 cups water (for cooking	1/2 cup sugar (or more to taste)
the rice)	1/8 tsp. vanilla extract
	Sweetened condensed milk

In a medium saucepan, cook rice in the water, stirring continuously. When rice is ready it will be slightly transparent. Stir in cocoa, sugar and vanilla. Let sit for 5 minutes. Top with a bit of sweetened condensed milk.

Mexican-American Traditions

*"Our father and mother gave us our lives, but
they also gave us a sense of pride and identity.
Our food is an expression of that pride."*

I f her father, Augustin, had not started a restaurant back
in 1979 Sandy Medina might today be a professional
drummer, touring, perhaps, with a salsa band, spending her nights in
happy, boisterous bars in the company of friends and colleagues who live
their lives with passion for their work and commitment to each other,
eating great food.

Every night would be a party.

Precisely because her father, Augustin, *did* start a restaurant,
Sandy Medina's life looks pretty much like I just described. She spends
her days and nights managing the happy and boisterous La Fonda El
Taquito, the nationally recognized Mexican restaurant and tavern on
Kansas City's Southwest Boulevard. La Fonda has twice been named one of
the top 50 Hispanic restaurants in the United States by Hispanic
Magazine. In 2001, the publication called it a Mexican version of the
popular television show "Cheers."

Every night *is* a party.

And the food *is* great. Not only would you be hard-pressed to find

Teresa Medina and Cynthia Souter check on the progress of the picadillo.
Above: Two of Teresa Medina's grandchildren: Brianna Casey and Gabriel Chesen.

better Mexican food anywhere else in Kansas City, you'd have to look far and wide to find better Mexican food this side of the Rio Grande.

And the drumming? Sandy Medina does that at night and on her days off. Down in her basement where she has set up a pair of congas, a pair of bongos and an awesome stereo.

"It helps me unwind after a long day," she says. "Sometimes I come

Before the Spanish invasion of Mexico in 1521, the native diet was based primarily on corn, supplemented with fruits and vegetables, including tomatoes, squash, sweet potatoes, avocado, coconut, pineapple, papaya and cactus. Game animals were also critical in the native diet. And Indian peoples had cultivated a tradition of growing and using a wide variety of chilies in their food.

During the Spanish colonial period, Mexican cooking was heavily influenced by Spain's culinary traditions. Spain's position as a world power and its commerce with nations around the globe brought olives, wines, spices, and exotic fruits to Mexico's shores. The Spanish also introduced domestic livestock and many advanced agricultural practices.

Mexico is a country now populated by three distinct groups: native peoples — descendants of the Aztec, Mayan and other Indian nations that originally inhabited the region; the descendants of the Spanish conquerors; and mestizos, who are descendants of both.

The mixing of cultures resulted in a mixing of cuisines, which, over time, became a single and formidable culinary tradition in its own right.

In the central Mexican state of Guanajuato, from which Augustin Medina immigrated, distinct Aztec and Spanish culinary traditions are both still in evidence, even after centuries of blending. Though one of the foods typical of the region — "mole poblano," a rich, dark sauce made with dried chilies, nuts, seeds, spices and cocoa — reflects a blending of both traditions.

Mexican food is now popular in virtually every corner of the world. It has become so commonplace in the United States that it is, for most families, no longer even considered "ethnic" food. As the percentage of the American population with Mexican ancestry increases over the next few decades, the influence of Mexican cooking traditions on mainstream American food will become ever more significant.

home and I'm just exhausted. Other times I'm all jazzed up with energy to burn. That's when I come down here and just start banging away."

Sandy Medina is explaining all this to me in a near shout, over shots of tequila at her cool glass-block wet bar in the basement of her lovingly-restored turn-of-the-century home. The salsa sounds coming from her stereo fill the room as her brother-in-law, Enrique Chaurand, and her nephew, Enrique's son, Juan-Carlos, go mano-a-mano on the drums, after a family dinner.

I use the word "family" in its largest sense. Sandy, her partner, Cathie Chesen, and son Gabriel, have been joined by Sandy's mother, Teresa Medina; sister Maria Chaurand and husband Enrique; brother Cris Medina and wife Mary; and sister Yolanda Casey and husband Mike. Counting aunts, uncles, cousins, nieces, nephews and assorted friends and associates there are about 40 people here enjoying Sandy's food and music.

"There's a pretty strong connection between food and music," Sandy says, smiling as she watches Enrique and Juan-Carlos go at it. "They're both ways to express what you're all about from the inside out."

This is what the late Augustin Medina had dreamed of. A big, happy family. Supported by the strong, successful businesses he worked so hard to establish.

Medina was born in Leon, Guanajuato, northwest of Mexico City. Leon is a city known for its beauty, its shoe industry, its passion for soccer, and its food. The guitar-picking, former professional soccer player moved to Kansas City in 1952, after marrying Teresa Garcia, who was born and grew up here.

For a time he worked in a meatpacking plant, all the while planning to someday open a restaurant.

"He liked to cook and he loved music," says Sandy. "So I think he wanted a place where he could offer both good food and good music. Plus, he wanted a business he could pass on to his children."

In 1978 Medina founded El Taquito, a now-thriving enterprise that makes corn tortillas for wholesale and retail markets. A year later he

Gabriel Chesen and his cousins Brianna and Mikaela Casey dig in at the kids' table. Below: Sandy Medina and her nephew, Juan-Carlos express themselves on the drums.

opened La Fonda.

Sandy remembers that in its early days, La Fonda was a hangout for neighborhood musicians. "I was pretty little, but I do remember teen-agers and old men bringing their guitars. And while my dad was making carnitas, they would be sitting around on crates and boxes playing and singing all these old Mexican folk songs. My father would sing, too. And sometimes he would stop cooking and play along on his guitar. I remember the sound and the feeling of it. That's what we try to create at the restaurant today. A warm feeling. A feeling of welcome."

All of Augustin Medina's children are actively involved in the family businesses. Cris Medina manages La Fonda on Friday nights. It's a far cry from his regular line of work. Cris is executive director of the Guadalupe Center, a community center and social service agency founded in 1919 to serve Kansas City's Mexican immigrant community. This position provides him with a unique perspective of Mexican-American

Mike and Yolanda Casey.

culture.

"Even as the Mexican-American population increases in size and is increasingly assimilated into mainstream American life, there are aspects of our culture that we maintain," Cris says. "Our food is one of those things that we hang on to. It reminds us of who we are and where we come from."

Cris' wife, Mary, agrees. "In Mexican culture, life revolves around family and food. Food helps bring the family together."

Yolanda, Sandy and Cris' sister, says she's trying to make sure that her children grow up with a strong sense of their Mexican identity. "For me it's important that our children be bilingual. Of course, I'm teaching them to appreciate our Mexican food traditions, and also how to make the food."

As Yolanda's daughters, Mikaela and Brianna grow, one of the things they'll learn is that that there are subtle, but significant differences in cooking traditions within the Mexican-American population from region to region across the United States.

Cris points out that Mexican-Americans in California will prepare certain dishes slightly different than how those same dishes are prepared in Texas, and that in Texas they will be different than in the Midwest. "Obviously, it's the same dish," Cris says. "But a lot depends on locally available ingredients. And then there's the influence of other cultures in each region. You'll see the differences in homes and in restaurants."

Cris notes that "Latino influence has permeated the nation's food service industry. That's a good thing, because in our culture it's not only important what is served, but also the way it is served. That's one of our contributions to the industry. We bring an attention to detail and presentation that has raised the quality level in American restaurants."

Apparently a few traditional Mexican dishes are so labor-intensive that they are sometimes saved for special occasions. Tamales, for example, are the ultimate in Mexican comfort food. But because they require so much time and effort, many families save them for Christmas and New Year's celebrations.

Teresa Medina points out that every Mexican cook makes tamales in her own way. "You can cheat and take shortcuts," she says. "But it's worth it to do it right. That why the holidays are always so special in our family. We have the tamales to look forward to."

Maria explains that chicken molé, another fairly complicated dish, is traditionally served at Mexican wedding receptions. "Dishes like these take on added meaning," she says. "Because they're associated with certain times. Tostadas are another example. In our family, we always had tostadas on our birthdays."

Cris chimes in. "Yeah. And frankly, I got a little tired of them."

His sisters laugh and nod. Cris keeps it going. "It was like, 'Please, Mom! Can't we just once have something else on my birthday? Anything! Please!' "

Maria says that her extended family pretty much does everything together. "You can never visit one or the other of us for just an hour. It'll always end up being a lot longer than that. And you better come with an appetite."

"It's true!" Sandy exclaims. "I'll invite someone over to watch a game on TV and before I know it, or can stop it, the whole family is here. So to be on the safe side, I always have plenty of food and beer on hand. Whenever possible, we make a party of it."

This evening has been proof of Sandy's preparedness. There has been plenty of food: shrimp cocktail, cactus salad, sopes and picadillo, enchiladas, frijoles charro, flan and rice pudding. And also plenty of beer.

Sandy, who's more than just a little sentimental, puts her arm around her mother's shoulders.

"Our parents gave us life," she says. "But they gave us so much more than that. They also gave us a strong sense of ourselves — who we are as individuals, who we are as a family. We Medinas, we know who we are."

Teresa Medina smiles at her daughter's words.

Cris Medina has established a Friday night tradition at La Fonda El Taquito. After the bar has closed and the customers and the DJ have gone home, Cris begins to play recordings of Mexican folk songs performed on acoustic guitar. The restaurant's employees and the Medina family and their friends gather around, pour a round of drinks, and they sing. And if you listen closely you can almost hear Augustin Medina, back there in the kitchen, singing along.

Sandy Medina and her mom, Teresa.

Medina Family Recipes
and other traditional Mexican dishes

Shrimp Cocktail Medina Style

1 lb. medium-size shrimp, shelled
and de-veined

1 box spicy shrimp boil
1 lemon

Boil shrimp in shrimp boil according to the directions on the box. Squeeze juice from lemon into cooking water. Do not overcook.

For the cocktail sauce:
1 small bottle ketchup
1 tbsp. horseradish
2/3 cup pickle relish

1 tbsp. Worcestershire sauce
Dash of bottled hot sauce (such
as Tabasco)
Juice from 1 fresh lime

In a mixing bowl combine all ingredients and stir until well blended. Vary amounts to taste.

For the pico de gallo:

3 tomatoes, seeded and diced	1 avocado, diced
1 bunch cilantro, chopped fine	Juice from 1 fresh lime
1/2 yellow onion, chopped very fine	Salt
1 large jalapeno pepper, stemmed, seeded, chopped very fine	Whole cilantro leaves for garnish
	Lime wedges

In a mixing bowl combine diced tomatoes, cilantro, onion, pepper, avocado and lime juice. Mix well. Season with salt and pepper to taste.

Spoon 2-3 tablespoons of cocktail sauce into the bottom of a cocktail glass. Spoon about 1 tablespoon of pico de gallo on top of the cocktail sauce. Arrange 4 shrimp around the edge of the glass. Garnish with cilantro leaves. Chill and serve with lime wedges on the side.

Cris Medina and his sister, Maria Chaurand

Fresh Cucumber Salad
Pepino Fresco

2 cucumber, peeled and sliced thin	1 jicama, cut in chunks
1/2 onion, sliced thin	2 fresh limes
2 ripe tomatoes, sliced thin	Salt
2 avocados, cut in chunks	Bottled hot sauce

In a medium-size salad bowl, layer vegetables, starting with cucumber slices, then onion, tomatoes, avocado and jicama, in that order. Squeeze limes over salad. Sprinkle with Mexican or kosher salt. Add hot sauce to taste.

Cactus Salad

1 jar (32 oz.) cactus (such as San Marcos brand), drained
1/2 bunch fresh cilantro, chopped

1 small red onion, halved and sliced thin
1 fresh tomato, seeded and diced

Thoroughly rinse cactus with cold water and drain well. In a mixing bowl combine cactus, cilantro, onion and tomato. Toss, chill and serve.

Queso Fundido

2 lbs. Queso Chihuahua (available at Mexican groceries)
1/2 chorizo, cooked and crumbly

1 cup, seeded diced tomatoes (optional)
Warm corn tortillas

Melt cheese in top pan of a double boiler. Stir in chorizo. Add tomatoes if desired. Spoon into warm corn tortillas and serve.

Angel Hair Pasta
Fideo

1 (12 oz.) package *fideo* (angel hair pasta)
2 tbsps. vegetable oil
2 cups chicken stock

1-2 cloves garlic, peeled
1/4-1/2 yellow onion, chopped
1 cup canned tomatoes, drained
Salt to taste

In a food processor, purée tomatoes, garlic and onion.

In a heavy skillet, sauté fideo in oil until pasta is lightly browned. Add puréed tomato mixture and bring to a boil. Reduce heat and let simmer for a few minutes. Add 1 cup stock and bring back to a boil. Reduce heat and let simmer until liquid is absorbed. Add another cup stock and bring back to a boil. Reduce heat and let simmer until pasta is tender. Do not cook dry. Add additional stock if necessary to achieve a nice soupy sauce.

Picadillo Medina Style

1 lb. ground chuck
1 (15 oz.) can whole tomatoes
2 cloves garlic
1/4 yellow onion, finely chopped

1 tbsp. whole cumin seeds
Salt
Freshly ground pepper

In a heavy skillet brown beef with a little of the chopped onion. In a blender or food processor purée tomatoes, onion, garlic and cumin seeds. Stir this mixture into ground beef and season with salt and pepper to taste. Bring to a boil, then reduce heat and let simmer for about 20 minutes. Option: Add one small can peas and carrots while simmering.

Little Corn Cakes
Sopes

2 cups masa harina flour (available
in the Mexican food section
of most groceries)

1-1/3 cups warm water
(Vegetable oil for deep frying)

In a mixing bowl, combine masa harina and water . Using your fingertips, working quickly and gently, knead dough until smooth. Divide dough into 12 equal parts and form 2 1-inch balls from each piece. Cover these with a damp kitchen towel to prevent the dough from drying out. One at a time, put each ball in a zip-lock plastic bag and using a tortilla press, flatten each ball into a 3-inch disk.

Lightly toast each disk (sopita) on a well-greased griddle or heavy skillet for about 3 minutes on one side and 3 minutes on the other, or until the dough is opaque and just beginning to brown.

After letting sopes cool briefly, yet while still warm, pinch the edges of each disk to form a ridge. Your sopes should now look like small, shallow, flat-bottomed bowls. Return the sopes to the griddle or skillet to fry for 2-3 more minutes. The sopes will still be slightly moist. Sopes may be served soft. However, usually sopes are deep fried before serving to achieve a crisper texture.

Fill with a scoop of hot picadillo and top with shredded lettuce, grated cheese and sopes sauce (recipe follows).

Sauce for Sopes

1 (15oz.) can whole tomatoes
1/2 yellow onion, chopped fine

1/2-1 tsp. whole oregano
Salt

In a food processor, purée tomatoes and garlic. Stir in onions and oregano. Season with salt to taste.

Mexican Rice Medina Style

1 cup medium grain rice
2 cups chicken stock
2 tbsps. vegetable oil or lard
1-2 cloves garlic, peeled

1/4-1/2 yellow onion, chopped
1 cup canned tomatoes, drained
Salt to taste

In a food processor, purée tomatoes, garlic and onion.

In a heavy saucepan, sauté rice in oil until rice is lightly browned. Add puréed tomato mixture, cover and bring to a boil. Reduce heat and let simmer for a few minutes. Add stock, cover and bring back to a boil. Reduce heat and let simmer until liquid is absorbed and rice is tender, about 15 minutes.

Enchiladas Caseras

1 cup or more vegetable oil	8-10 corn tortillas
For the sauce:	2 cloves garlic
8 Ancho chilies	Salt to taste

Remove stems and seeds from chilies. In a saucepan, cover chilies in water and bring to a boil. Let simmer until chilies are soft. Drain. In a food processor, purée chilies and garlic. Add some of the cooking water to the purée as necessary to make a smooth paste. Season with salt to taste.

For the filling:	1 medium yellow onion,
6 potatoes, peeled and diced fine	chopped fine
1/2 lb. chorizo, casing removed	2 cups shredded Colby cheese

In a saucepan, cover potatoes with lightly salted water and bring to a boil. Reduce heat and let simmer until potatoes are tender. In a heavy skillet, cook chorizo over medium-high heat until thoroughly browned and crumbly. Add potatoes, stir, cover and keep warm. In a mixing bowl, combine cheese and onion. Mix thoroughly.

For the topping:	3-4 cups freshly grated Parmesan
3-4 cups shredded iceberg lettuce	cheese or Mexican white cheese

In a deep skillet or electric frying pan, bring oil to medium heat. On at a time, dip tortillas in sauce then place in oil. Turn quickly and remove.

Spoon 3-4 tablespoons of potato and cheese/onion fillings onto the middle of the tortilla. Roll filled tortilla quickly. Top with lettuce and cheese. Serve immediately. May be topped with some of the sauce if desired. If enchiladas are to be served later, keep covered and warm in a 200-degree oven until serving.

Frijole Charros

Cold water	1 small yellow onion, peeled
1 lb. dry pinto beans	and quartered
	Salt

Sort and rinse beans. In a stockpot cover beans with plenty of cold water and bring to a boil. Reduce heat, add onion, cover and let simmer until beans are tender. Drain, preserving some of the cooking water for making gravy. Season with salt to taste.

Using a potato masher, mash beans a bit to create a thicker sauce. The object here is not to mash the beans into a paste, but simply to break them up a bit, which will release some of the natural starch in the beans to make a thicker gravy. Leave them more whole than not. Use some of the cooking water to achieve a soupy, not-too-thin-not-too-thick consistency.

1/2 lb. chorizo
4 strips bacon, chopped
1/2 yellow onion, chopped fine
2 chilies guajillo, seeded and
    chopped

1 large ripe tomato, seeded and
    diced fine
2 tbsps. vegetable oil
1/2 bunch cilantro, chopped fine

In a heavy skillet, cook chorizo and bacon until chorizo is browned and crumbly. In a separate skillet sauté tomatoes, onion and chilies until onions are translucent. Combine beans, chorizo and bacon, tomato mixture and cilantro in a large saucepan and simmer for 30 minutes.

Palomitas
A yummy summer drink

Fresh lime
1 1/2 oz. premium white tequila
Squirt soda
Juice of 1/2 lime

Spearmint leaf
Mexican salt
Slice of lime or orange

Apply fresh lime around rim of glass and dip rim in salt. Add 1-1/2 oz. of premium white tequila. Fill the glass with ice. Fill glass with Squirt brand soda. Squeeze half a fresh lime into the drink. Add fresh spearmint leaf and a dash of Mexican salt. Garnish with slice of lime or orange.

Yolanda brings a plate of cactus salad to the table.

Flan Napolitano

Ana Casas, a waiter at La Fonda, makes this delicious dessert for the restaurant's customers. It's one of the best things I've ever tasted.

1 can condensed milk	1 tbsp. vanilla extract
1 cup whole milk	4 eggs
1 (8 oz.) package cream cheese	3 tbsps. sugar

In a heavy saucepan, heat sugar over medium-high heat. When sugar begins to melt, reduce the heat to medium. Continue to cook, stirring continuously, until sugar is melted and browned. Immediately pour over the bottom and sides of a shallow baking dish. A fluted custard mold or a 9-inch pie pan work well for this purpose. Set aside and let caramelized sugar cool.

Preheat oven to 350 degrees.

In a food processor, blend condensed milk, whole milk, cream cheese, vanilla and eggs for about 3 minutes. When caramel is cooled, slowly pour the blended ingredients into the baking dish.

Place the baking dish in a larger baking pan, then pour hot water into the larger pan halfway up the sides of the baking dish.

Bake about 45 minutes or until an inserted knife comes out clean. Cover flan loosely with foil if necessary to prevent excessive browning.

Remove from oven and chill in refrigerator at least 3 hours. To serve, run a knife around top edge and invert flan onto a serving plate.

Rice Pudding
Arroz con Leche

This rich and delightful recipe is from Teresa Garcia Medina, Sandy Medina's mother.

1 cup whole grain rice	1 can evaporated milk
1 stick cinnamon	1 small can condensed milk
1/2 cup sugar	1/2 cup raisins (optional)
2 cups water	

In a medium-size saucepan, combine rice, cinnamon stick, sugar, salt and water. Bring to a boil. Reduce heat and let simmer until rice is cooked and water is absorbed, about 20 minutes. Add evaporated and condensed milk and bring back to a boil. Reduce heat and let simmer until pudding is thickened, about 10 minutes. Stir in raisins, if desired. Remove cinnamon stick. Serve with powdered cinnamon sprinkled on top.

The following are not Medina family recipes but do reflect Mexican and Mexican-American culinary traditions

Fiesta String Beans

3 lbs. fresh green beans, trimmed
3-4 tbsps. vegetable oil
2 yellow bell peppers, cored, de-veined and cut in long, thin strips
4 red jalapeno peppers, cored, de-veined and cut in long, thin strips

1 yellow onion, halved and sliced thin
8 cloves garlic, halved lengthwise
1 cup slivered almonds
Salt
Freshly ground pepper

Boil green beans in salted water until just tender. Drain immediately in a colander and then immediately plunge beans into a large bowl or pot of ice water. This will stop the cooking process and keep beans crisp and bright green. When beans are chilled, drain and set aside.

In a large heavy skillet, sauté sliced onions and garlic halves over medium heat until they begin to caramelize. Add peppers and continue to cook until peppers are just tender. Add green beans and increase heat. Cook just until green beans are warmed through. Season with salt and pepper to taste. Stir in slivered almonds and serve hot.

Nachos with Creamy Cheesy Shrimp

2 cups grated pepper jack cheese
1 (8 oz.) package cream cheese, softened
1 cup sour cream
3 cloves garlic, chopped fine
1 bunch green onions, chopped fine
1 lb. shrimp, peeled, de-veined, boiled and coarsely chopped
2 tbsps. chopped fresh cilantro

1 tbsp. fresh lime juice
1/2 tsp. ground cumin
1-1/2 tsps. ground red pepper, or more to taste
1 cup grated extra-sharp cheddar cheese
Salt
Freshly ground pepper
Big bag of tortilla chips

Preheat broiler. In a mixing bowl, combine grated pepper jack cheese, cream cheese, sour cream, garlic, shrimp, onions, chopped cilantro, lime juice, ground cumin and red pepper. Season with salt and pepper to taste. Spread tortilla chips on a baking sheet. Spoon cheese and shrimp topping over chips. Broil until cheese topping begins to brown. Remove and sprinkle with grated cheddar cheese. Return to broiler until cheddar cheese melts.

Mexican Pesto

1 cup, packed, fresh cilantro leaves
2 tbsps. pine nuts
3 cloves garlic

1/2 cup freshly grated Parmesan
   cheese
2 tsps. fresh lemon juice
1/4 cup extra-virgin olive oil

In a small skillet, toast pine nuts over medium heat until golden brown. Combine pine nuts and all other ingredients except olive oil in a food processor. On lowest setting purée the ingredients while drizzling oil in through the top of the cover. Scrape sides and continue until well blended. Serve tossed with angel hair pasta, on tortilla chips, or as a condiment.

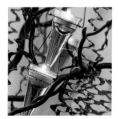

Chilaquiles
A good way to use day-old tortillas.

8 *stale* corn tortillas
3/4 cup canola oil
1 (15 oz.) can diced tomatoes,
   liquid reserved
2-3 jalapeno peppers, stems
   trimmed
2 cloves garlic, peeled
1/2 small yellow onion, chopped
   very fine

2 tbsps. fresh oregano, chopped
1/2 cup grated Monterey jack
   cheese or a white Mexican
   cheese
1/2 cup cream
1 bunch green onion, chopped fine
Salt to taste

Cut the tortillas into 1-inch squares. In a heavy skillet, fry the tortilla squares in the oil until crisp and golden. You may need to do this in batches. Drain on paper towel. Discard all but 2 tablespoons of the oil.

In a food processor, purée the tomatoes, peppers, garlic, onion, oregano and salt. Add some of the liquid from the canned tomatoes if necessary to achieve a nice, smooth consistency.

In the skillet, bring the tomato sauce and reserved oil to a boil. Reduce heat and let simmer for about 5 minutes. Gently stir in the fried tortilla chips and remove from heat. Pour cream over the top, then add grated cheese and green onions. Place skillet under the broiler to melt cheese. Serve hot with refried beans.

Teresa, Cynthia Souter, Maria and Yolanda prepare the enchiladas.

Stuffed Jalapenos

12 large jalapeno peppers
1 (8 oz.) package cream cheese,
   softened
2 cups shredded jack cheese

6 cloves garlic, chopped fine
1 bunch scallions, chopped fine
1 tsp. cumin
24 slices bacon (perhaps more)

Preheat oven to 300 degrees.

Cut tops off peppers and remove seeds and veins from inside each pepper. In a mixing bowl, combine cream cheese, jack cheese, garlic, scallions and cumin. Mix thoroughly. Fill each pepper with cheese mixture. Wrap each stuffed pepper with two slices of bacon. Wrap the first slice around the pepper lengthwise, sealing the open end. Wrap the other bacon slice the other way around. Secure bacon with toothpicks if necessary.

Place wrapped peppers on baking sheet and bake for about 30 minutes.

Rebecca's Guacamole

4 ripe avocados, peeled and pitted
2 cloves garlic, chopped fine
1/3 cup cilantro, chopped fine
1 tbsp. lime juice

2 tsps. chipotle powder
1 cup canned tomatoes, diced
   and drained
Salt to taste

Combine all ingredients except tomatoes in medium mixing bowl and mash thoroughly with potato masher. Stir in tomatoes. Adjust seasonings. Serve with tortilla chips or as an accompaniment to an entrée.

Patata Fuerte

8-10 potatoes, peeled and diced
1 (32 oz.) jar cactus (such as San
   Marcos brand), drained
4 red jalapeno peppers,
   stemmed, de-seeded and
   de-veined
1/2 large red onion, sliced thin

3 cloves garlic, chopped fine
2 tbsps. fresh lime juice
2/3 cup fresh cilantro, chopped
2/3 cup cider vinegar
1 tbsp. sugar
Salt
Freshly ground pepper

Cook potatoes in boiling salted water until just fork tender. Drain in a colander and immediately plunge potatoes into a large bowl of ice water to stop the cooking process. When completely chilled, drain potatoes and set aside.

Cut peppers into long, matchstick-size pieces.

In a large mixing bowl, combine all ingredients and gently turn and stir until mixed well. Adjust seasonings. Serve as a salad.

Huevos Diablo

6 hard-boiled eggs, peeled
3 tbsps. mayonnaise
2 tsps. cayenne pepper
1 (4 oz.) can diced green chilies,
   drained

2 tsps. sugar
1 tbsp. cider vinegar
Paprika

Carefully slice eggs in two lengthwise. Remove yolks and in a mixing bowl combine yolks, mayonnaise, chilies and vinegar. Mash yolks and then mix well with other ingredients, except paprika, until smooth. Fill each egg half with an equal amount of the yolk mixture. Sprinkle a little paprika on top of each. Chill and serve.

Mexican Meat and Potatoes

3 lbs. stewing beef, cubed
1 yellow onion, chopped fine
Bacon drippings
1 (15 oz.) can stewed tomatoes,
   drained
2 cups bottled pickled jalapenos,
   drained

3 cloves garlic, chopped fine
2 lbs. potatoes, peeled and cubed
1 cup beef stock
2 tsps. cumin
Salt
Freshly ground pepper

Brown beef and onion in bacon drippings. Add tomatoes, jalapenos, garlic, potatoes, stock and seasonings. Cook over low heat until meat is tender.

Marinated Steak Fajitas

1 lb. sirloin steak
4 cloves garlic, peeled
6 jalapeno peppers, stems trimmed
1/2 yellow onion, peeled
1 cup red wine vinegar
1 bottle dark beer

2 tsps. salt
1/2 tsp. pepper
1 tsp. oregano
1 tsp. cumin seeds, crushed
1 tsp. ground red chili pepper

In a food processor or blender, purée the jalapenos, garlic, onion, vinegar, beer and seasonings. Cut the meat into 1-inch cubes and place in a large bowl. Cover with the marinade. Marinate for about 8 hours or overnight.

Start a fire in a kettle-type grill, such as a Weber. Use pure lump charcoal. Meanwhile, soak some chunks of mesquite in water. When the charcoal is covered in a fine gray ash, put some of the mesquite chunks on the coals and put the grill on the kettle.

Skewer the steak pieces with grilling skewers and place on the grill. Cook medium-rare (just pink inside). Serve in warm flour tortillas with grilled onions and peppers.

Flan and (in background) rice pudding.

Chorizo
Mexican Sausage

2 lbs. ground pork
2 tbsps. paprika
1 tsp. pepper
1 tsp. ground oregano
1 tsp. ground cumin
1/4 tsp. ground coriander

2/3 cup cider vinegar
1 tsp. garlic powder
2 tsps. onion powder
2 tbsps. salt
2 tbsps. chili powder

Combine all ingredients in a large mixing bowl. Mix thoroughly until smooth and well blended. Refrigerate in an airtight container for two days before using.

Stuffed Beef Tenderloin

Tell your butcher you are going to stuff the tenderloin and have him butterfly it for you.

4 lbs. tenderloin, butterflied
1 lb. chorizo (recipe above)
4 cloves garlic, chopped fine
1 medium yellow onion,
    chopped fine
1 cup breadcrumbs

1 cup chopped spinach, cooked
    and drained
1 cup dried apricots, diced fine
1 cup pine nuts, lightly toasted
1 egg, slightly beaten
Salt
Freshly ground pepper

Preheat oven to 325 degrees. In a heavy skillet over medium-high heat, cook chorizo, garlic and onion until chorizo is completely browned and crumbly.

In a large mixing bowl, combine chorizo mixture — including any rendered fat — with breadcrumbs, spinach, apricots, pine nuts and egg. Season with salt and pepper. Mix thoroughly.

Lay the butterflied tenderloin open and flat on a work surface. Spoon chorizo filling along one edge of the tenderloin. Starting with this edge, roll up tenderloin jellyroll style. Tie the roll with butcher's string every 3-4 inches along the roll. Bake in an uncovered roasting pan at 325 for at least 1-1/2 hours until meat thermometer inserted in the center of roll reads 140 degrees. Let rest for 10-15 minutes before slicing. Slice 1-inch thick. Garnish with cilantro leaves.

Brianna and Mikaela Casey.

Chocolate Chicken

3 lbs. chicken pieces, skin on
1/4 cup vegetable oil
1/3 cup dried apricots, diced fine
1/3 cup candied oranges, diced fine
2 cloves garlic, chopped fine
1/2 tsp. dried cumin
1/4 tsp. nutmeg
1/4 tsp. ground cloves
1 medium yellow onion, chopped fine
1/4 tsp. cinnamon
1 orange bell pepper, cored and diced (green bell pepper may be substituted)

1/2 tsp. salt
1/4 tsp. white pepper
2 large ripe tomatoes, peeled, seeded and diced
Grated rind of 1 lemon
2 tbsps. fresh lime juice
2 squares. bitter chocolate, chopped
2 tbsps. chili powder, more or less to taste
2-1/2 cups chicken stock
1/4 cup orange liqueur
1/2 cup whole cashews

In a heavy skillet or ovenproof pot, sauté onions in oil over medium heat until onion is soft and translucent. Add chicken; brown pieces on both sides. Remove and set aside. Preheat oven to 350 degrees.

In the skillet sauté garlic, bell pepper and tomatoes over medium-low heat for about 10 minutes. Stir in seasonings, lemon rind, lime juice, apricots, orange, liqueur and stock. Bring to a boil. Reduce heat, cover and let simmer for another 30 minutes. Then add chocolate pieces, stirring until melted. Taste test sauce and adjust seasoning if necessary.

Return chicken to skillet and cover with sauce. Cover and bake for 1 hour, or until chicken is tender. Sprinkle with cashews. Serve immediately.

Catfish Caliente

4 catfish fillets
2 cups buttermilk
3 cups yellow cornmeal
1 tbsp. chili powder
1 tsp. garlic powder
1 tsp. onion powder

1 tbsp. sugar
1 cup vegetable oil
Salt
Cilantro leaves
Lime juice

Rinse catfish fillets and pat dry with paper towels. Place fillets in an airtight plastic container and cover with buttermilk and refrigerate for 3-4 hours. In a shallow pan mix together cornmeal and seasonings. In a heavy skillet or an electric frying pan heat oil to medium-high. Dredge catfish fillets in cornmeal mixture. Fry until golden brown on both sides. Squeeze a bit of fresh lime juice over each fillet before serving. Garnish with fresh cilantro leaves.

Picante Puerco
South of the Border Pork Barbecue

6-8 lbs. bone-in Boston pork butt	trimmed
2 cups cider vinegar	8 cloves garlic, crushed
1 cup ham stock	1/2 yellow onion, chopped fine
1 cup unsweetened pineapple juice	1/2 tsp. cumin seeds
	1 tbsp. sugar
3 chipotle peppers, stems	Salt to taste

Slow-smoke a bone-in Boston butt in a wood/charcoal-burning barbecue pit at 235 degrees for 10-12 hours until internal temperature of butt reaches 205 degrees.

While the meat is cooking, in heavy saucepan combine stock, pineapple juice, chipotle peppers, garlic, onion, cumin seeds, sugar and salt. Bring to a boil. Reduce heat and let simmer for 1 hour. Remove from heat and pour through a fine mesh strainer into another saucepan. Let peppers, garlic and onion cool. When cooled, cut pepper pods open lengthwise and remove seeds. In a food processor purée peppers, garlic and onion with a few tablespoons of the sauce.

Push purée through strainer into sauce and bring back to a boil. Remove from heat. Let cool and adjust seasonings to taste.

When butt has reached 205 degrees remove from smoker, wrap tightly in heavy foil and let sit for 30 minutes. Unwrap butt, and pull the meat into shreds. In a large mixing bowl thoroughly combine the pork and the sauce. Serve in warmed tortillas.

Bunuelos
Fried Cookies

4 eggs	1 tsp. salt
1/4 cup sugar	1 cup sugar
1 tsp. vegetable oil	1 tsp. ground cinnamon
2 cups flour	1 cup vegetable oil (for frying)
1 tsp. baking powder	

In a large bowl combine eggs with 1/4 cup sugar and beat until thick and lemon-colored. Add tsp. oil. In a separate bowl combine 1-1/2 cups flour, baking powder and salt. Gradually add flour mixture to egg mixture. Beat well.

On a floured work surface, knead dough thoroughly, incorporating the remaining 1/2 cup flour, until dough is smooth.

Shape dough into 18 balls. Roll each ball into a disk about 4 inches wide. Let rest uncovered on waxed paper for about 10 minutes.

Heat oil in a heavy skillet or electric frying pan to medium. Fry disks until golden brown, turning once. Drain on paper towels. Sprinkle with mixture of 1 cup sugar and 1 tsp. cinnamon.

Native American Traditions

*"It wouldn't be fair to say everything in
Osage culture revolves around food, but nothing
much happens in Osage culture without it."*

Guilt is a rotten appetizer. Like, perhaps, many European Americans, I experience a certain amount of retroactive guilt in the presence of Native Americans. And there's nothing like self-reproach to ruin one's appetite.

Thank God, therefore, for Ray Red Corn. Not only did he salve my White Guilt with the warmth of his welcome, he fed me well.

Raymond W. Red Corn III is an Osage Indian and a damn fine cook, which, I am led to believe, is a redundant statement. When I arrive at his house for dinner, Ray is working the deep fat fryer — tongs a flyin' — making a mess of fry bread. Before he even says hello, he tweezes a warm piece of fry bread out of a basket and drops it in my hand.

"Here," he grins. "Try this."

I have never before tasted fry bread.

And what a shame. It's delicious.

No. Wait. That doesn't describe it.

It is plain. It is simple. Delicate and substantial. Crispy and chewy. Light and rich. Foreign and familiar. Flour, water and oil. Sugar, salt and

Above: Alex Red Corn.

Before the early 1800s, the region that is now the Kansas City metropolitan area was inhabited by Kansa Indians. However, after Lewis and Clark paved the way for pioneers from the eastern United States, these Native Americans were compelled to leave the region under terms of a treaty with the federal government.

In 1828, representatives of the Osage people, a tribe that had long been based in Missouri, ceded rights to the land that eventually became Jackson County to the United States government. Soon white settlers from the East arrived to buy cheap land and the foundation for what eventually became Kansas City was established.

Ten years later, Shawnee, Delaware and Wyandot Indians arrived in the area as a result of the Indian Removal Act, which displaced them from their traditional regional homes. Indians from the Miami, Ottawa, Kickapoo, Potawatomi, Wea, Peoria, Iowa, Sac and Fox tribes also came to the area.

According to tribal histories, the Osage people originally descended from the Oneonta, a tribe living in central Missouri in the mid-14th century. The name "Osage" is a corruption of the word Wa-Zha-Zhe, which is how the people referred to themselves.

By 1830s the Osage had been relocated, to the territory that eventually became Oklahoma. During the early 20th century the Osage were among the wealthiest people in the world because of the oil and gas drilling rights on their reservation.

Ray Red Corn says that in the early 20th century many Osage bought expensive china and flatware. Today, Osage dinners are frequently served on these heirloom dishes.

Though the Osage were highly skilled hunters of buffalo and other wild game, they were also accomplished farmers, growing squash, corn and beans in fields around their permanent settlements. These became the fundamental elements of Osage cooking. When, after the 1870s, they were forced onto reservations, federal government food commodities also became an integral part of the Osage diet.

Thanks to Terri Baumgardner for her reporting on Red Corn Native Foods.

baking powder. Shortening and a century-and-a-half of history.

It's like a fritter, like a tortilla, like a waffle, like a doughnut, like a funnel cake, like bread, like manna.

Ray Red Corn explains: "Before the Europeans arrived, native tribes had vastly different diets. The woodland Indians ate differently than did the Indians on the plains. And the Indians of the Pacific Northwest ate differently than the Indians of the desert. They were different peoples living in different places.

"But after the United States government forced Natives onto reservations a process of culinary homogenization began. And one example of this was the distribution of food commodities, like flour and oil, to the reservations. Most reservations were supplied these basic foodstuffs as part of a subsistence diet. And let's be honest, there's not much you can do with these commodities, except make fry bread.

"Now it's a matter of tribal and family pride. All Indians, no matter where they're from, are convinced that their fry bread is best.

"They're all wrong, of course," Ray laughs. "Because the truth is that Osage fry bread is the best."

Ray Red Corn is wearing a red apron monogrammed with the Osage word Ha-pah-shu-tse, which literally translated means "corn that is red."

"Make sure you get a picture of this apron," Rays instructs the photographer. Besides being his family name, the word on his apron is also the name of his company. Besides being an Osage, Ray is an entrepreneur who understands the value of free advertising. His business is Red Corn Native Foods and one of his products is fry bread mix.

⋈⊷◆⋈⊷

Ray lives with his four sons — Ryan, Jon, Alex and Studebaker (Raymond Michael) — in Kansas City's Lenexa suburb. Their blond, blue-eyed looks are not at all what you'd expect a Native American family to look like.

Ray Red Corn explains: "My father is half Osage and my mother is a non-Indian. And my wife was not an Indian."

"But DNA isn't really what it's all about anymore," Ray says. "It's as much about commitment as blood. It's more about how you define yourself than how your blood defines you.

"The Osage are defined by their history, their stories, their

Raymond W. Red Corn III.

traditions, their culture and their love and commitment to one another and to their community. That and their food."

Ah! Their food.

Osage food is straightforward and assertive. It's like Ray in that regard. As he brings heaping platters and steaming bowls of traditional Osage dishes to the table he tells me that, generally, Osage food is seasoned only with a little salt and pepper.

"We tend to let the food speak for itself," he says.

Apparently the food has spoken well of itself on previous occasions. Ray's sons, their girlfriends and Geoff Bahr, a family friend, happily help themselves.

The menu tonight includes corn soup, Osage meat pies, a hominy and pork stew, Osage squash and, of course, fry bread. My favorite is the squash, sweet as honey, translucent, with a glowing amber color and a rich caramel flavor. It's like candy from the garden.

"It's a little strange for me to serve these dishes around a table like this," Ray says. "This isn't the usual context for this kind of food. Typically we'd eat these things at a traditional Osage feast. For us a 'small' feast is 35 to 50 people. And the 'committee' dinners average 400 to 450 people. And they're all served sit-down style, all at once.

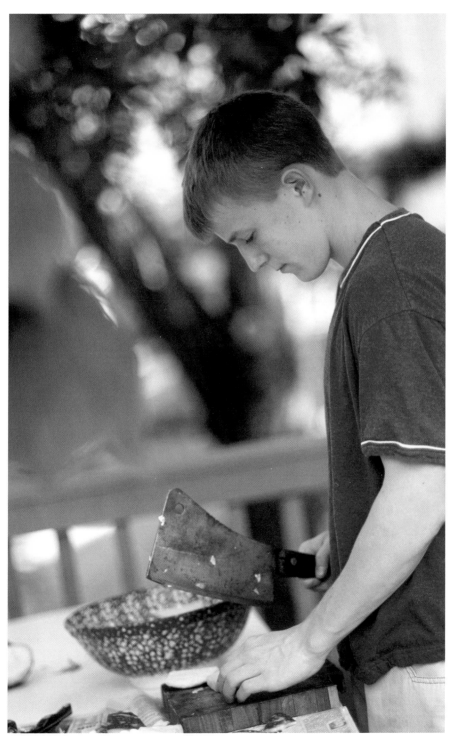

Studebaker Red Corn preparing Osage squash.

"As you can imagine, cooking for and serving that kind of crowd requires a lot of planning, coordination, skill and experience. In Osage culture, cooking is a team sport."

And the team captain is a woman.

The head cook for Osage feasts is considered so important that a tribal committee is given responsibility for appointing a person — always a woman — to the position. It is a high honor to be named to this post and usually comes after years of apprenticeship and experience.

It's hard work. These cooks are entrusted with organizing and staffing crews that will feed 40-50 people three meals a day for four days straight at cultural events held in neighboring Osage districts. These are typically held at encampments away from home, with only running water, "rations," some shade and firewood provided by the host camp.

Cooking conditions and resources are better when feasts are held in one's own district, but then that's where the aforementioned dinners for 400 people are held.

⋑⋸◆⋑⋸

As Ray explains these things, I am struck by his enthusiasm and good cheer. Clearly, it is his nature to be so, but he might be forgiven some sadness, given that it was only a year ago that his wife, Libby, died of cancer.

"Libby was a rare gem," Ray says. "Beautiful, quiet and long-suffering, with a reliable stubborn streak. She was very protective of her boys. She really loved 'em good.

"Libby left us with the same grace she possessed while living. I'd rather celebrate that she lived than dwell on the loss."

Death, birth, rites of passage and the celebration of significant achievements are all cause for feasting in Osage culture. A child's first birthday and the initiation of a young man to the ceremonial dance are frequently occasions for special meals. And a year after a person's death, friends of the deceased's family may give a feast to mark the end of mourning.

"It wouldn't be fair to say everything in Osage culture revolves around food," says Ray. "But nothing much happens without it. We're big on ceremony, and almost all our ceremonies include eating. There were 250 people at my father's 90th birthday party. That was some feast."

The Red Corn name has been passed to Ray through four generations. His father, Raymond W. Red Corn Jr., is an ordained Southern

Baptist minister and the co-founder, along with his wife, Waltena Red Corn, of the business that Ray now owns and operates. His grandfather was Raymond W. Red Corn Sr. and his father, who did not have an English surname, was Wy-e-glah-in-kah, which in Osage means "Bravery Before Sense."

Perhaps it takes more bravery than sense to try to make a living selling fry bread mix, or to live and raise sons in the disparate worlds of a culturally homogeneous Kansas City suburb and the Osage Nation. But Ray Red Corn seems entirely at ease with the challenge.

It would be trite to say he's "proud" of his heritage. It's not like being Osage is something he's achieved, like a high school varsity letter or a job promotion. Pride is something one wears. Being Osage is not that. It's just what he is.

"Folks have lots of preconceived ideas of what we're about," he says. "But my advice is get to know your Indians one at a time. Because anything you think you know about us needs to be checked out in person."

Communicating to the wider world what Native American, specifically Osage, culture is all about is something of a mission for Ray. And the vehicle for his mission is food. Specifically corn.

"My father kept a strain of traditional Osage Red Corn growing for 60 years in his back yard on the reservation," Rays says. "He was keeping something precious and rare alive for future generations."

"This entire food culture — Indian corn, fry bread and the way we prepare it — has been hidden away on reservations and in clans for the last 100 years," Ray says. "And unless somebody specifically went out looking for it, they'd never find it. I'm trying to change that."

∋∈◆∋∈

The day after our dinner, Ray Red Corn sends me an e-mail message to explain something.

"Thank you," he says, "for dining with us last night. In Anglo culture the guest thanks the host for the dinner. But with the Osage it's the other way around. In Osage culture the host thanks the guest for the honor of their company and for the privilege of serving them. So, thank you."

That's nice, Ray. But, after all, I am Anglo. Thank *you*.

Jon and Studebaker Red Cor, with Me-Nah, which means "daughter" in Osage.

Red Corn Family Recipes
and other traditional Native American dishes

Fry bread was perhaps the most delightful surprise of all the foods I tasted while writing this book. The fry bread Raymond Red Corn makes is crispy and gold on the outside, ever so slightly chewy and snow white on the inside. Fry bread is the one recipe I hope all readers will try at least once. I know it is destined to become a family favorite in the Worgul house.
Ray Red Corn's mother, Waltena Red Corn, is not Indian. But by all accounts she has perfected Indian cooking and has earned the respect of Osage cooks for her wonderful, airy, golden-brown fry bread. Though there are as many authorities on fry bread as there are Indians on any given reservation, here is some of Waltena's own wisdom on the subject:

"First of all, there are as many different types of fry bread as there are fry bread cooks. At every opportunity, sample fry bread from different tribal nations and different clans within these nations to discover which you like best.

"Fry bread is relatively easy to make. There are, however, a few tips first-time fry bread makers should keep in mind.

"Maintaining the proper moisture content is critical. I have found that it's easier to achieve the proper moisture balance if I mix by hand. When properly mixed, fry bread dough will be a bit 'wetter' than most bread dough. Add water gradually as you mix by hand. As a test, I like to fill my hand with dough above a bowl, flatten my hand, fingers together and palm vertical (as if ready to give a stiff handshake). If the dough immediately falls off my hand, it's too wet. If it doesn't fall off at all, it's too dry. When the dough has the proper moisture content the dough will 'crawl' off your hand slowly and drop back into the bowl.

"Patience is a virtue. If you must mix your dough and fry it immediately, you will get satisfactory results. If you can mix the dough 2-4 hours ahead of your frying time you'll get better results. For the best possible results mix your dough the night before. Your bread will be lighter and more pleasing to the eye.

"After mixing, while the dough is quite wet, it may be put in a plastic bag and refrigerated until needed. This is especially convenient when preparing large quantities.

"Perhaps the second most important thing to remember when making fry bread is to knead the dough lightly and roll it to a proper thickness.

"Sprinkle a good amount of flour on your work surface and rub some on your rolling pin. But during the actual kneading process try to get as little flour on the bread dough as possible. Knead lightly using your fingertips. Turn your dough over just a few times, getting only enough flour on the dough to prevent your rolling pin from sticking to it.

"Roll out your dough no thicker than a lady's pinkie finger. The Osage women who taught me how to make fry bread used butcher knives to cut the dough into individual pieces. In commercial preparation we used a pizza cutter for speed. The size of the piece is up to you. The fry bread served at Osage feasts is about 3-by-5 inches, before frying. Most folks like it around 3-by-3 inches.

"As you pick up each piece of dough, stretch it slightly before dropping it in the oil to fry. This step is considered by most Osage fry bread masters to be most important. This is where you can compensate for having rolled your dough a little too thin or a little too thick. Pieces that are too thick can be stretched a little thinner. Pieces that are too thin should be barely stretched at all.

"You should be pleased if, when frying the bread, it 'poofs up' so much that you can't

Studebaker and Jon Red Corn.

get it to turn over to fry on the other side. This doesn't happen on every piece, even for experienced feast cooks, but when it does, you know the bread will be light and tasty and attractive on the table.

"A good thermometer is the most accurate way to tell if your cooking oil is the correct temperature. The way experienced Osage cooks tell is to watch how long it takes the bread to come back to the surface after it's been gently dropped in the oil. Usually 4-5 seconds is about right. If it stays at the bottom much longer than that, your oil is not hot enough. Keep in mind that placing several pieces in the cooking oil in rapid succession will cool the oil temporarily, so judge its temperature by the first few pieces of bread.

"Finally, if your bread is flat and won't rise at all during frying, you may not have enough water in your dough. You may also have rolled or stretched the dough too thin.

"If your fry bread is doughy in the center, even though the outside is golden brown, your frying oil may be too hot. The dough may also be too thick.

"If your family and friends insist that you make fry bread more often, well, that's a problem we can live with."

Fry Bread

4 cups Ha-pah-shu-tse Indian Fry Bread Mix (or other fry bread mix)	1-1/2 cups warm water Vegetable shortening or lard Flour

In large mixing bowl combine water and fry bread mix. Stir with wooden spoon or mix with hands until well blended. Let stand 30-40 minutes. The longer it stands the lighter the bread. Heat shortening to 350-375 degrees in a deep-fat fryer or a skillet at least 1-1/2 inches deep. On floured work surface, knead lightly with fingertips. Roll dough no thicker than your thumb and no thinner than your pinkie. Cut into 3-inch squares. Gently pull and stretch each piece, then carefully drop into the hot oil. Turn when the underside is golden-brown. When golden brown on both sides, remove and drain on paper towel. Do not puncture. Serve warm with butter, honey or powdered sugar.

Indian Taco Bread

Mix dough as if for fry bread. Divide dough into 8 equal balls. On a floured work surface, roll out each ball to 1/4-inch-thick disk. Cut 2 slits in the center of each disk and fry as directed for fry bread, without pulling or stretching the dough. Top with taco filling (recipe follows) or chili, shredded lettuce, grated cheese and salsa.

Indian Taco Filling

This isn't a Red Corn recipe. It's mine. But it tastes great on Indian Taco Bread.

1 lb. ground chuck
1/2 lb. ground pork
3 tbsps. bacon fat or lard
1 medium yellow onion,
    chopped fine
5 cloves garlic, minced

Salt
Freshly ground pepper
Red pepper flakes
Ground cumin
1 cup spicy V-8 vegetable juice

Melt bacon fat or lard in heavy skillet. Over medium heat cook chopped onion until beginning to turn golden brown. Add meat and cook until crumbly and completely browned. Add garlic, then season with salt, pepper and spices to taste. Then stir in vegetable juice, reduce heat and simmer until thickened.

Grape Dumplings

2 cups fry bread mix
3/4 cup warm water

48 oz. grape juice
1/2 cup sugar

In a large mixing bowl combine fry bread mix with warm water. Mix with wooden spoon or hands until dough is smooth. On a floured work surface, roll dough to about 1/8-inch thick — half the thickness of a pencil. Cut into approximately 2-inch squares. Combine grape juice and sugar in saucepan and bring to a boil. Drop dumplings into boiling juice, reduce heat to medium and simmer approximately 30-40 minutes or until juice thickens. Gently stir occasionally. Serve warm.

Osage Meat Pies

2 lbs. Ha-pah-shu-tse Indian
    Fry Bread Mix
Flour for work surface
2 lbs. coarsely ground chuck

1 cup finely-diced kidney suet
1 tbsp. pepper
1 tbsp. salt
1 cup water

Kidney suet is available any butcher or meat processing facility. Chill the suet in the refrigerator or freezer before use. Suet is much easier to work with when it's frozen or cold. Slice off 1-inch chunks and peel off the thin transparent skin. Discard the stringy parts that come off with the skin. Once the suet has been skinned, chop it into very small pieces.

Prepare the fry bread dough with a little less water than usual, which will make the dough a little stiffer than for fry bread. Set dough aside.

With your hands mix the ground chuck, suet, salt, pepper and water, making sure to break up any large chunks of suet while mixing. The suet needs to be evenly distributed throughout the meat.

On a floured work surface make a lemon-sized ball of dough. Knead lightly, then roll it out into a circle about 8-9 inches in diameter, about the thickness of a piecrust. Make an egg-shaped meatball from 1/2 cup of the meat mixture and place it in the center of the dough. Fold the dough over the meat. Along the edge of the meat, press the dough together with your fingertips. Use a knife or pizza cutter to cut away excess dough leaving about 1/4.-1/2 inch border along the seam. Place the pie seam side down on a greased baking sheet. Repeat until all meat is used, about 8-9 pies. Don't let your meat pies touch each other on the baking sheet. Brush the tops of the pies with vegetable oil. Bake for 20 minutes at 425 degrees. Remove and cool on a rack for 10-15 minutes, then wrap loosely in foil until serving.

Geoffrey Bahr, a family friend and silversmith.

Osage Squash

Ray says this recipe always results in a fight over the last few pieces when it's served at family reunions.

1 Hubbard squash (large, bumpy grayish green) or, alternatively, 1 crookneck squash (large and white, with green stripes)	5 lbs. sugar 2 lbs. butter or margarine A bit of water

Wash the outside of the squash thoroughly. You will be leaving the rind on. Cut off the stem tip and discard. With a cleaver or large heavy knife, cut the squash in half and remove the seeds and stringy insides. Cut the squash in pieces about 3 inches square (or in triangles as necessary).

You'll need a fairly large pot for this recipe, or two smaller pots will do.

Cover the bottom of the pot with one layer of squash pieces, rind side down. Place the remaining pieces in the pot in layers rind side up. Add about 2 cups of water, then the sugar. All of it. Add the butter and cover the pot. Cook over medium heat for about 3 hours. Do not stir. Just let it cook. When the squash has turned a deep translucent amber, it's ready. The juice from the squash will have mixed with the sugar and butter to make a medium-bodied syrup, which will have nearly covered all the pieces.

When done, gently remove each piece using tongs or a large spoon. Place squash on a serving platter rind side down. Serve warm.

Steam Fry

For Kansas Citians this recipe should become a favorite because, like barbecue, making it involves a fire. Ray says steam fry is the trickiest of the Osage meat preparation techniques, but also the most rewarding when done correctly. Since he says he's never seen it made on a stovetop, we recommend making it on top of a coal/wood-burning kettle grill, such as a Weber.

Start with a pork shoulder or Boston butt. Carefully separate all fat, bone and tissue from the meat. Cut the resulting "clean" pieces of pork into chunks about 1-1/2 inches square. The size isn't as critical as the uniformity of the pieces.

Your cooking pot should be heavy and large. A long rectangular stainless steel serving pan works quite well. A cast-iron Dutch oven will also work, though it may be a bit small.

Make a charcoal fire in your grill using a starter chimney or a paraffin fire starter. Do not use lighter fluid. Let the coals burn until they are just covered in a light-gray ash. Grease your pan with vegetable shortening, then set it on the grill and let it heat up a bit. Do not, however, let it get so hot that the shortening begins to smoke. Fill the pan with cubed meat to a depth of 2-4 inches. If your pan is the right temperature, things should start sizzling right away.

Stir the meat every few minutes while it browns. The natural juices from the meat will start to flow and will accumulate in the bottom of the pan. Continue to stir every 5-8 minutes. As the liquid cooks off, add water once, about 1/2-inch or so. When your fire is right, the pan juices will be simmering strong and steady. Add charcoal briquettes as necessary to maintain your fire.

While cooking, season the meat with salt and pepper to taste.

After about an hour, begin to test the meat by removing a piece and pressing on it. When it comes right apart, or if you begin to notice meat coming apart as you stir, it's ready. This isn't North Carolina "pulled pork." You don't want it shredded. As Ray's family friend, "Aunt" Mary, a full-blood Osage, used to say: "Don't stir it too much — our people want to know what they're eating." Ideally the meat will be ready at just about the same time that the liquids have cooked almost completely away, leaving the outside of the meat with a nice browned appearance and the inside soft and moist.

Serve with fry bread, soup or stewed root vegetables.

Hominy
Posole

2 cups hominy, soaked in water or chicken stock overnight
1 lb. Boston butt pork roast, or country style pork chops

Chicken stock
Salt
Freshly ground pepper

This is a simple recipe. And in the Osage tradition, nothing more than salt and pepper is added to the hominy and pork. The straightforward flavors of the two ingredients blend and complement each other nicely and need little in the way of adornment.

Put the roast in a stockpot and add the pre-soaked hominy and enough stock to cover the meat. Salt and pepper to taste. Bring to a boil, then reduce heat and let simmer 3-4 hours, until hominy is tender.

Variations on this basic recipe include the addition of all or any of the following: finely chopped onions, minced garlic, diced carrots, jalapeno peppers, chopped mustard greens or chopped spinach.

This is one dish that actually benefits from crock-pot-style slow cooking overnight (10-12 hours) on the low setting. Cooking the posole using this method does not require soaking the hominy overnight.

The following are not Red Corn family recipes, but reflect some of the cooking traditions of Plains Indians, with a few liberties taken. Forgive me, Ray.

Pumpkin and Sunflower Seed Soup

1 large yellow onion, chopped fine
4 tbsps. sunflower oil
3 qts. chicken stock
1 (15 oz.) can pumpkin
2 cups hulled sunflower seeds, pureed
1 bunch green onions, green parts chopped fine
4 cloves garlic, minced

3 tbsps. butter
1 cup heavy cream
2 tbsps. maple syrup
Salt
Freshly ground pepper
Ground sage
2 cups fresh sweet corn cut from cob (canned corn an acceptable substitute)

In a stockpot, cook the onions in sunflower oil until golden brown. Add chicken stock and bring to a boil. Lower heat and add canned pumpkin, stirring until thoroughly incorporated. In a food processor, puree sunflower seeds into a peanut butter-like paste, then add to soup. Stir thoroughly until sunflower seed paste is completely incorporated. Add remaining ingredients. Season with salt, pepper and sage to taste. Bring back up to a boil and remove from heat. Serve warm with cornbread and applesauce.

Cranberry Sauce for Buffalo Roast

Buffalo meat is increasingly available in supermarkets and retail butcher shops. However, if you can't find buffalo meat at your local grocer, this sauce also makes a fine accompaniment for beef roast.

1 bag whole cranberries	1 small yellow onion, chopped fine
1 cup sugar	3 tbsps. sunflower oil
3 cloves garlic, minced	2 tbsps. butter
1 cup water	Salt
1 cup (or more) dry red wine	White pepper

In a large saucepan, add the cranberries, sugar, garlic, water and the wine. Bring to a boil, then reduce heat and let simmer for about ten minutes. Meanwhile, in a small saucepan, saute the onion in sunflower oil until golden brown, then add to the cranberry mixture. (As the cranberries cook they will pop. This is my favorite part.) Cranberry sauce thickens naturally. Add more wine or water if necessary to achieve desired consistency. Salt and pepper to taste. Serve warm, melting the butter in the sauce just before serving.

Rabbit with Peanut Pepper Sauce

2 lbs. rabbit meat, cut in pieces on the bone	1 small yellow onion, chopped fine
6 tbsps. peanut oil	3-4 cups chicken stock
1 medium yellow onion, chopped coarse	3 cloves garlic, minced
1 sweet red bell pepper, chopped coarse	1 cup chunky-style peanut butter
	Salt
	Freshly ground pepper
	Cayenne pepper

Season the rabbit pieces with salt and pepper. Then, in a heavy skillet, brown the rabbit in four tablespoons of oil. When rabbit is nicely browned, add chicken stock, coarse chopped onions and bell pepper and bring to a boil. Reduce heat and let simmer.

Meanwhile, in a medium saucepan, saute finely chopped onion in 2 tablespoons of oil until it just begins to caramelize. Add about 1-1/2 cups of chicken broth from the cooking rabbit. Add garlic and bring to a boil. Add peanut butter and stir until completely incorporated. Add cayenne pepper to taste. Thicken sauce if necessary with a little more peanut butter. Thin sauce if necessary with a little more stock. Serve rabbit with onions and peppers and peanut pepper sauce on top.

Raymond M. "Studebaker" Red Corn.

Succotash in Rosemary Cream Sauce

2 cups fresh shelled lima beans
2 cups fresh corn, cut from cob
1 red bell pepper, diced fine
2 tbsps. butter for sautéing
    vegetables
2 tsps. fresh parsley, chopped
3 tbsps. scallions, chopped fine

2 cups chicken stock
2 tbsps. butter for sauce
2 tbsps. flour
1/2 tsp. dried rosemary
1 cup heavy cream
Salt
Freshly ground pepper

Boil beans in salted water about 20-30 minutes until tender. Drain. In a small skillet, cook corn and diced pepper in butter over medium-high heat for about 5 minutes. Add the cooked beans, parsley and scallions, stir and remove from heat.

In a medium saucepan, melt butter over low heat. Gradually stir in flour to make a roux. Gradually add chicken stock and bring to a boil. Add rosemary, reduce heat and let simmer for about 5 minutes. Salt and pepper to taste. Add cream and stir in vegetable mixture. Serve warm.

Raymond W. Red Corn III wearing a broadcloth blanket with bead strip.

Mixed Greens with Pork and Peppers

5 lbs. mixed fresh greens, such as
    collard, mustard and even
    spinach
1 bunch green onions, chopped,
    including white parts
2 smoked ham hocks
1 red bell pepper

1 yellow bell pepper
6 cloves garlic, chopped
2 qts. (or more) chicken stock
Salt
Fresh ground pepper
Cayenne pepper

Thoroughly wash greens. Trim stems.

In a large stockpot, boil ham hocks and garlic in about 2 quarts of chicken stock. Season with salt, pepper and cayenne to taste. Let simmer for about 4 hours. Add greens and green onions and add enough additional chicken stock to cover greens. Bring to a boil. Reduce heat and let simmer for 1 hour. Add more chicken stock if necessary.

Core peppers and remove seeds. Cut peppers into matchstick-sized pieces. When 30 minutes cooking time remains, add peppers to greens. Serve warm with plenty of ham hock pieces in each serving.

Indian Risotto

Of course, risotto is an Italian dish. But this recipe uses squash, which is an ancient Native American food. Besides, maybe, just maybe, the indigenous peoples gave Christopher Columbus the recipe for risotto and he took it back to Italy.

2 acorn squash	1 cup dry white wine
2 cups arborio rice	6-8 cups chicken stock
1 medium yellow onion,	1/2 cup Romano cheese
chopped fine	Salt
4 tbsps. peanut oil	Freshly ground pepper
3 cloves garlic, minced	

Cut squashes in half, remove seeds and place on cookie sheet or in shallow roasting pan. Roast in oven at 350 degrees until squash is quite tender, about an hour. Remove from oven. Let cool. Scoop squash from shell and place in a bowl.

In medium saucepan, bring chicken stock to a boil. Reduce heat, cover and keep simmering while making the risotto. In a large saucepan, over medium heat, cook onions in peanut oil until they have begun to caramelize. Add rice; stirring to coat all grains with oil. Cook for about two minutes, stirring continuously. Ladle 1/2 cup of hot chicken broth into the rice. Continue to stir and cook until all liquid has been absorbed. Adjust heat to keep rice mixture simmering. Continue to add stock, about 1/2 cup at a time, stirring constantly.

After 2 to 3 cups of stock have been added and absorbed, stir in the cooked squash and the garlic. Next add add the wine and stir until absorbed. Then continue adding stock 1/2 cup at a time, stirring constantly until rice is tender, with just a slight firmness. Add cheese and salt and pepper to taste and stir until cheese is melted. Serve immediately.

Chipotle Pintos and Hominy

3 cups dry pinto beans
3 cups Indian hominy
3 chipotle peppers
4 cloves garlic, chopped
8 slices bacon, chopped

1 small yellow onion,
    chopped fine
3 quarts apple cider
Salt
Freshly ground pepper

Sort and rinse beans and hominy, then soak overnight in water or chicken stock. Drain. In a stockpot cover the beans, hominy, chipotle peppers and garlic with apple cider. Season with salt and pepper. Bring to a boil, then reduce heat and let simmer for 2-4 hours, or until beans and hominy are tender. After cooking, remove chipotle peppers. These may be discarded or, if you like more spicy heat, trim and discard stems, chop peppers and return to pot.

In a small skillet cook chopped bacon and onions until bacon is crisp. Add bacon, onions and bacon fat to beans and hominy just before serving. May be served over rice.

Roasted Turkey Breast with Cranberry Butter and Sage Gravy

1 whole turkey breast (6-8 lbs.)
1 lb. butter
4 cloves garlic
1 cup dried cranberries
2 medium yellow onions,
    quartered
3 large carrots, cut in 1-inch
    pieces

3 celery stalks, cut in 1-inch
    pieces, include leaves
1 tsp. rubbed sage
Salt
Freshly ground pepper
4 tbsps. butter
4 tbsps. flour
4 cups chicken stock

Preheat oven to 350 degrees. Wash turkey breast under cold running water and pat dry with paper towel. In a small saucepan, cover dried cranberries with water, bring to a boil and cook for about 5 minutes. Drain. In a food processor, thoroughly combine butter, garlic and cranberries. Starting on the outside edges of the turkey breast, gently but firmly push your fingers under the skin of the breast, working your way toward the center, creating pockets on either side of the breast. Then, using your fingers, evenly distribute the butter mixture into these pockets. Push on the outside of the breast to spread the butter evenly between the skin and the meat.

Place the breast, skin side up, in a shallow roasting pan. Cover and surround the breast with the onions, carrots and celery. Roast the turkey for about an hour and a half, or about 10 minutes per pound. After an hour, start checking the internal temperature of the meat with a meat thermometer. When it reads 160 degrees, it's done. Remove the turkey to a platter along with the vegetables.

Place the roasting pan over a burner on your rangetop. Over medium-low heat, melt the butter, stirring and scraping the caramelized juices and bits of meat and vegetables off the bottom of the pan. When butter is melted, gradually add the flour, then the sage, stirring to make a smooth roux. Gradually add the chicken stock and bring to a boil. Let gravy bubble for 1 minute.

Serve turkey and gravy with hominy, or corn and cranberry cakes (below) or rice.

Corn and Cranberry Cakes

4 cups dried corn	1/2 tsp. salt
1 cup dried cranberries	Buttermilk
1/2 cup sugar	Lard or bacon fat for frying

Using a food processor grind corn medium coarse. In a large mixing bowl, combine corn, cranberries, sugar and salt. Add just enough buttermilk to moisten the corn mixture, allowing you to make small round cakes, about the size of your palm, no more than 1/2-inch thick. The cakes should not be too moist, only moist enough to keep them from falling apart. Fry in lard or bacon fat until golden brown on both sides. Serve with maple syrup.

Corn Pudding

1/2 cup yellow cornmeal	1 tsp. salt
4 cups whole milk	1/4 tsp. cinnamon
1/2 cup maple syrup	1/4 tsp. ginger
1/4 cup light molasses	1/4 tsp. nutmeg
2 eggs, slightly beaten	1/4 tsp. cloves
4 egg yolks	1 (15 oz.) can corn, drained
2 tbsps. butter, melted	1/2 cup whole milk, cold
1/3 cup brown sugar	

Preheat oven to 300 degrees. In top of double boiler, heat 4 cups milk. Slowly stir cornmeal into hot milk. Cook about 20 minutes, stirring continually. Butter 9-by-9-inch baking dish. In a mixing bowl, combine remaining ingredients, except cold milk. Stir in cornmeal mixture and mix well. Pour into buttered baking dish, then pour cold milk on top. Do not stir. Bake uncovered for about 2 hours, or until just set. The top will quiver when shaken. Be careful not to overbake. Let rest 30 minutes before serving. Serve warm. May be served with a little bourbon drizzled on top.

Cornbread Pudding

1 dozen day-old cornbread muffins	1 tsp. cinnamon
1 qt. heavy cream	1/2 tsp. nutmeg
6 eggs, slightly beaten	2 tbsps. light molasses
1 cup sugar	1 tsp. vanilla extract
	1/2 tsp. salt

Preheat oven to 325 degrees. Break cornbread muffins into small pieces and place in a buttered medium-size casserole or 9-by-13-inch baking dish. In a large mixing bowl, stir together cream and slightly beaten eggs. Add remaining ingredients and mix gently but thoroughly. Pour over the crumbled cornbread and let sit until the cream/egg mixture is well absorbed by the cornbread. Bake until firm, about 60 minutes.

Berry Cobbler

1 cup fresh or frozen blackberries, blueberries or raspberries	1/3 cup buttermilk
	2 tbsps. butter
1/2 cup brown sugar	1 egg, plus 2 egg yolks, lightly beaten
2 tbsps. honey	1 tsp. vanilla extract
1 cup yellow corn meal	1/2 tsp. salt

Preheat oven to 375 degrees. Combine sugar, honey, buttermilk, butter, eggs, egg yolks, vanilla and salt. Add cornmeal to make a batter. Butter a 9-by-9-inch baking dish. Add berries and several tablespoons of honey. Pour batter over the berries. Bake for 35 to 40 minutes. Cool and serve with heavy cream.

Sweet Potato Cakes

4 large sweet potatoes, peeled and quartered	1 tsp. cinnamon
	1/2 tsp. salt
2 eggs, plus 3 egg yolks, slightly beaten	1/2 tsp. nutmeg
	1/2 tsp. cayenne pepper (more or less to taste)
1 cup flour	
1 tbsp. sugar	

Boil the sweet potatoes until tender. In a large mixing bowl, mash the sweet potatoes, then stir in the remaining ingredients. Form small cakes, about the size of your palm, no more than 1/2-inch thick. Fry in vegetable shortening until crispy on both sides. Serve with maple syrup.

Finally, after our dinner Ray Red Corn told me a funny story that he says illustrates Osage humor at it dryest. It inspired me to come up with one last recipe for this chapter.

"During the Depression it was not at all uncommon for the Osage to get meat wherever it could be found. Game was still plentiful in the Osage Hills in those days and fishing was not recreation, but a way to put food on the table.

"Some of the younger Osage men, my father included, had taken to running troutlines (pronounced 'trot-lines' in Osage country). This involved the stringing and baiting of a line of hooks across a creek or pond in the evening, then returning in the morning to harvest the catch, usually catfish.

"My mother was in the kitchen with Aunt Mary one morning when the fisherman returned. Aunt Mary was a kind woman, a full-blood Osage. After my mother and father married, she took my mother under her wing and generously shared her knowledge of Osage feast traditions.

"Aunt Mary looked out the window and saw that one of the boys was carrying a snapping turtle of some size by its tail — which, by the way, is the only safe way to carry a snapping turtle. Aunt Mary immediately instructed my mother to turn the oven up to 400 degrees. When my mother asked why, Aunt Mary revealed that the oven was the snapping turtle's immediate destination. 'Are you sure, Aunt Mary?' my mother asked, wide-eyed. 'Won't he just bang around in there?'

"Without looking up and with no hint of a smile, Aunt Mary answered, 'Not for long.'"

Snapping Turtle Stew

2 lbs. snapping turtle meat, cut in 1-inch cubes (*I have no clue where one might actually buy snapping turtle meat. But as I understand it, if you have a valid fishing license in most states it's legal to catch 'em.*)

2 medium yellow onions, chopped fine

3 tbsps. peanut oil

3 stalks celery, chopped, include leaves

1 qt. chicken stock

1 cup dry kidney beans, soaked overnight in chicken broth

2 cups fresh sweet corn, cut from cob (canned corn is an acceptable alternative)

4 cloves garlic, peeled and chopped

1 (15 oz.) can diced tomatoes, undrained

3 tbsps. maple syrup

1 cup dry white wine

Salt

Freshly ground pepper

In a stockpot, brown turtle meat and onion in peanut oil. Add chicken stock and all remaining ingredients. Salt and pepper to taste. Bring to a boil. Reduce heat and simmer, uncovered, until turtle meat is quite tender, about an hour. May be served over rice or on top of Indian Taco Bread.

Jewish Traditions

*"An artist paints to express who he is.
A cook cooks to express who she is."*

Pella Fingersh's children wrote notes to her on the pages of her cookbooks. "Have a nice day, Momma." "I like my birthday present, Mom." "I love you, Mother." They knew that leaving notes in her cookbooks was a sure thing. There was no doubt she would find them there.

These many years later she finds them still. She'll be paging through a thumb-worn cookbook in search of an old, forgotten recipe, and suddenly there it is. A message from the past. A reminder and remainder of love.

"Here. I can show you," she says. She goes to a bookshelf in the corner of her kitchen and returns with an old volume barely held together with tape. She flips through the pages.

"There. That one is from my son Paul." She touches the fading, childish script with her fingertips.

Pella and her husband, Jack, live in Prairie Village, Kansas.

Pella is a native of Israel. She met Jack on a blind date in 1962 when she was touring the United States after completing her service in the Israeli

Left: A berry tart, one of Pella Fingersh's specialties. Above: Pella's mother, Esther Jochnowitz.

The Bible describes Israel as the "land of milk and honey." Yet most Americans know little about Israeli cuisine and have perhaps only a vague idea of what Jewish cooking is about.

In the United States, the Jewish foods most familiar to non-Jews are those associated with specific holiday traditions. For example, it is generally well-known that latkes — potato pancakes — are eaten at Hanukkah.

The other thing most associated with Jewish cooking is the set of biblical dietary laws known as Kashrut that dictate to practicing Jews which foods may be eaten and how they are to be prepared. These include prohibitions on certain foods. Pork, rabbit and shellfish are forbidden. And dairy products must be cooked and eaten separately from meat. "Pareve" foods such as fish, eggs, fruits and vegetables may be eaten with either meat or milk.

But Jewish cooking is more than just a collection of holiday novelty dishes and religious rules and regulations.

In the first century B.C., Jews revolted against Roman occupation of Israel, resulting in Jews being banished from Jerusalem and Judea. Under Byzantine rule (324-640 A.D.), anti-Jewish laws were enacted forcing many Jews to leave the Middle East altogether. This trend continued and by the time of the Crusades, in the 11th century, only a few thousand Jews still lived in Israel.

The Jewish population had been dispersed throughout the world. And the culinary influences of the nations where Jews eventually settled is now reflected in Jewish cooking customs.

In Israel, Jews returning after the founding of the nation brought with them the food traditions of Eastern Europe, Russia and America. These have now been incorporated into the Israeli culinary identity.

And, despite the enmity that persists between Israel and its Arab neighbors, the food traditions of Morocco, Lebanon, Egypt, Syria and Jordan have heavily influenced Israeli cuisine. Even Palestinian cooking traditions have been incorporated into Israel's culinary identity.

Israel is, after all, a sophisticated, affluent Mediterranean nation. It is natural that its food would reflect the historical, political and geographical influences that formed the country itself.

army. One thing led to another, they got married and had three children.

The Fingersh home is understated and elegant, appointed with beautiful, compelling original artworks. Clearly, creativity is valued in this household.

This becomes even more evident as the Fingershes' dinner guests arrive.

The first to show up are Tiberius and Carla Klausner. Tiberius Klausner is a world-class violinist and the former concertmaster of the Kansas City Symphony. Carla is a professor of history at the University of Missouri-Kansas City, specializing in the Modern Middle East, medieval Europe and Judaic studies.

Next is Roger Kraft, the architect who redesigned and remodeled the Fingershes' house and who has recently participated in the restoration and expansion of Kansas City's Freight House and Crossroads art and entertainment districts.

Last to arrive is Irene Bettinger, a neurologist at St. Luke's Hospital.

Representatives of all points on the art-to-science spectrum of creative/intellectual pursuit would seem to be present tonight.

Jack, an attorney, gathers his guests for drinks beside the pool, in the shadow of a large sculpture by the late Kansas City artist Dale Eldred.

Small talk is quickly dispensed with. Almost immediately the group is deep in discussion regarding the search for a new symphony conductor.

When I first called Pella to talk about her participation in this cookbook project, she warned me. "I'm not a typical Jewish cook," she cautioned. "I'm not your Jewish grandma with her latkes and chicken soup."

I was intrigued. "Tell me more," I urged.

"Well, first of all, most traditional Jewish cooking in the United States originates in Eastern Europe," Pella explained. "But I grew up in Israel. So my cooking has been influenced by Jews from around the world who came to live in Israel. I can cook all the usual favorites, if you want me to. But mine is a much more eclectic style of Jewish cooking."

That cinched it as far as I was concerned. We scheduled dinner.

Dr. Irene Bettinger.

Back poolside, the discussion group is getting hungry. They're in luck. Pella calls from the kitchen door that dinner is ready. In no time the party reassembles on a balcony overlooking the pool and the terraced garden.

Pella's first course is a chilled cherry soup.

Pella's mother, Esther Jochnowitz, a native of Hungary, is seated opposite me. "This is Hungarian," she tells me. "This reminds me of my childhood."

Tiberius Klausner nods. He is also from Hungary. He is seated next to Esther and the two of them speak in Hungarian to one another throughout the evening.

The cherry soup is cheery and bracing. Tart, sweet, bright and deep. Pella stands behind me and watches as her guests spoon up the soup.

"I add a little kirsch to it," she says. "That makes it special."

Around the table, heads bob. It is special. But no one says so. They're all slurping.

Pella smiles and turns to go back to the kitchen.

"When you're ready, you can come get the rest of your dinner," she says over her shoulder.

In the kitchen, laid out on the countertop, are a golden challah, a platter piled with crispy kreplach, a pineapple and cheese kugel that looks to

Pella Fingersh concentrates on last-minute dinner preparations.

be the very definition of comfort food, and a majestic stuffed breast of veal.

Pella waves her hand in the general direction of the challah, kreplach and kugel.

"So, here are some classic Jewish dishes," she says. She laughs. "So maybe I am your Jewish grandma after all."

Roger Kraft looks admiringly at the food before him. "You can be my grandmother any day," he says.

When we are all seated at the table again, I sense that my moment for a "big question" has arrived. These people are a captive audience. They are hostages of Pella's food.

"So," I ask, "how is cooking like playing the violin, or designing a building, or practicing medicine, or lawyering?"

"Oh, cooking and music are very much the same," says Tiberius Klausner. "First, both cooks and musicians must learn basic technique. Then when you have mastered the fundamentals you begin to improvise and interpret."

Roger Kraft accepts the challenge and weighs in with his comparison of cooking and architecture.

"There are some obvious parallels," he says, leaning back sipping his wine. "First, there's an apprenticeship and a time when both a cook and an architect are mentored. This is when they begin to learn the 'vocabulary' of their craft. This is when they learn the range of combinations and possibilities available to them — how certain things go together, or don't."

At first, Carla Klausner isn't sure that teaching and cooking are in any way alike. But after a few more bites of veal she comes around.

"I think that imagination plays a big part in both," she says. "Mastery of your subject is necessary if you are going to be any good at it. And both are very personal."

Irene Bettinger, the doctor, doesn't compare cooking with medicine as much as she uses her training in neurology to diagnose cooking.

"In my experience," she says, "cooking is an art. Therefore it's a right-brain activity. Baking, however, is more science, and therefore it's left brain."

I look at Jack Fingersh, expecting witty and insightful comparisons of lawyering and cooking. But he's having none of it.

"OK, all you smart guys," he says. "You did good. Now shut up and enjoy your food."

The group complies.

"I'm not a social cook," says Pella. "I can't cook and talk at the same time. I can't answer the phone when I'm working in the kitchen. For me cooking is an art. For me it takes concentration."

Pella's mother, Esther, takes up this theme. "An artist paints to express who he is and what he feels and sees. A cook cooks to express who she is."

As I happily consume Pella's works of art, I ask her to describe the role of food in Jewish culture. But she cannot answer. She's now concentrating on dessert, a chunky applesauce with strawberries, a blackberry tart and another tart with dark chocolate and mixed berries.

But Irene Bettinger has heard the question and offers an opinion. "Food is at the heart of Jewish culture. It's one of the primary ways we affirm our traditions and identity. It brings us together."

Pella steps outside her kitchen door to pick some fresh mint leaves from her herb garden to use as a garnish on her dessert and to flavor the tea she is brewing.

"I actually started a kitchen fire the first time I cooked breakfast for Jack," she says.

Dr. Bettinger and I howl in delight.

"I was a newlywed," she says. "And I wanted to cook him an all-American breakfast. But I was Israeli — what did I know about all-American breakfasts? So I started by cooking some bacon in butter. And I wanted it to be nice and crispy, so I turned the heat on the stove to high. Well, it caught on fire. It was quite a mess."

Pella still remembers the first entire meal she made from scratch — Spanish chicken, a wild rice mold with cloves, and a strawberry glacé pie.

"The recipes are in that cookbook I showed you," she says. "Look. Here they are."

She flips through the pages. And there in the margin is a note. one of her little ones has drawn a heart and written a note. It says "Thank you, Mom."

Tiberius Klausner, Irene Bettinger and Esther Jochnowitz are entertained by their host, Jack Fingersh.

Fingersh Family Recipes
and other traditional Jewish dishes

Cold Cherry Soup

Pella serves this with a dollop of sour cream on top, garnished with leaves of fresh mint.

40 oz. frozen sour cherries	5 tbsps. cornstarch
8 cups water	1/2 cup kirschwasser (cherry
1-1/4 cups sugar	liqueur), or to taste
2 cinnamon sticks	

In a saucepan bring water and cherries to a boil. Cover, reduce heat and let simmer for 20 minutes. Dissolve cornstarch in a couple of tablespoons of water and slowly stir this into the cherry mixture. Bring back to a boil while stirring continuously until soup is clear and has thickened. Add liqueur. Chill completely before serving.

Kreplach

For the filling:
2 cups chuck roast, cooked
    and chopped
2 large yellow onions, chopped fine
3 cloves garlic, chopped fine

1 egg, slightly beaten
1 tbsp. olive oil
Salt
Freshly ground pepper

In a heavy skillet sauté onion until translucent. Drain oil. Add meat, garlic and egg and mix well. Season liberally with salt and pepper.

For the dough:
1 egg
1/8 tsp. salt

2/3 cup flour
Olive oil
Vegetable oil for frying

Beat egg slightly. Stir salt into flour and stir gradually with egg to form dough. Knead until dough is smooth and elastic.

On a lightly floured work surface roll dough into a thin sheet. Cut dough into 2-inch squares. Place a tablespoon of filling in the center of each square. Fold dough over, one corner to the opposite corner, to form a triangle. Press edges firmly together. Drop the kreplach into salted boiling water and cook for about 20 minutes. Remove from water and drain on towel. Brush with vegetable oil. In a heavy skillet add vegetable oil to a depth of about 1 inch. About 10 minutes before serving, fry kreplach in oil over medium-high heat, until kreplach are crispy and golden brown on both sides. Drain on paper towels.

Pella sets out a salad.

Challah

1-1/2 tbsps. dry yeast	1 tbsp. honey
1/2 cup warm water	4 eggs, slightly beaten
1/3 cup sugar	2 cups raisins
1/2 stick butter	6-1/2 cups flour
1 cup milk	1 egg
2-1/2 tsps. salt	Sesame seeds

Dissolve yeast in the warm water. In a saucepan heat milk and butter over medium heat until butter is melted. Pour this into a mixing bowl. Add sugar and salt. Let cool. Stir in the 4 beaten eggs. Add yeast and stir gently. Gradually add flour. Turn dough onto a lightly floured work surface and knead until dough is smooth and elastic, about 10 minutes. Place dough in a buttered bowl, put bowl in a warm draft-free place and let dough rise until doubled in volume, about 1-1/2 hours. Then punch dough down and let rise again until doubled in volume.

Preheat oven to 375 degrees.

Punch dough down once more. Fold raisins into dough. Divide dough in half. Roll each half into a cylinder about 1-inch thick and fold into an upside-down U-shape. Braid the legs of the U into the classic Challah loaf. Place the loaves on a baking sheet and let rise again until doubled in volume. Brush loaves with a mixture off an egg beaten together with a tablespoon of water. Sprinkle loaves with sesame seeds. Bake for 40-50 minutes.

Chunky Applesauce with Strawberries

5 lbs. Fuji or Delicious apples, peeled and cut into 1-inch chunks	5 (10 oz.) packages frozen sliced strawberries in syrup

Combine apples and strawberries (with syrup) in a saucepan. Cover and cook over medium heat until apples are tender.

Stuffed Breast of Veal

When you buy your veal, tell your butcher that you're going to prepare it stuffed and ask him to cut a pocket in the breast for the stuffing. It's easier for him to do it than for you to do it at home.

3/4 lb. ground chuck
3 (10 oz.) boxes frozen chopped
    spinach, thawed and
    squeezed dry
1 cup breadcrumbs flavored with
    Italian herbs
2 large yellow onions, chopped fine
4 cloves garlic, chopped fine
1/2 lb. smoked beef sausage, fully

cooked, chopped fine
8 eggs, slightly beaten
Seasoned salt
Freshly ground pepper
1 breast of veal
1 tsp. garlic powder
1 tsp. dried oregano
1 tsp. dried rosemary
1 tsp. dried thyme

Preheat oven to 325 degrees.

In a heavy skillet cook the ground chuck, onion and garlic until the beef is thoroughly browned and crumbly and the onion is translucent. In a large mixing bowl combine beef mixture with cooked spinach, breadcrumbs, sausage and eggs. Season with salt and pepper. Mix well. Stuff the veal breast with this mixture. Use skewers to close the veal breast opening. You may also tie it closed with butcher's string. Rub the outside of the veal breast with salt, pepper, garlic powder and dried herbs. Roast for 2-1/2 hours. Let rest 15 minutes before carving.

Blackberry Tart

For the graham cracker crust:
1-1/2 cups graham cracker crumbs

6 tbsps. melted butter
1/4 cup sugar

Combine cracker crumbs, sugar and melted butter in a mixing bowl. Mix well. Press into a 9-inch pie pan. Bake crust in a 350 degree oven for about 20 minutes. Let cool.

For the filling:
2 pints blackberries, hulled,
    washed, drained and dried

1/2 pint heavy cream
1/2 cup sugar
10 oz. currant jelly

Whip cream with sugar until cream is stiff. Spread enough whipped cream on baked graham cracker crust to completely cover the crust. Place blackberries on top of whipped cream. Liquefy currant jelly in microwave oven and let cool. Brush liquefied jelly on top of blackberries. Chill tart for 2 hours before serving.

Pella Fingersh's golden, crispy kreplach.

Pella's Hummus

2-1/2 (15 oz.) cans chickpeas,
    drained and rinsed
1/2 cup tahini (sesame seed paste)
6 cloves garlic
1/3 cup extra-virgin olive oil
2 tbsps. fresh parsley, chopped

2-3 tsps. cumin
1/2 tbsp. cayenne pepper
Juice of 3 lemons
Salt
Freshly ground pepper
Coriander to taste

In a food processor, puree all ingredients. Taste and adjust seasonings. Serve with toasted pita bread wedges.

The following are not Pella Fingersh's recipes, though they do reflect Jewish and Israeli cooking traditions.

Cannellini Dip

1 (15 oz.) can white kidney beans
    (cannellini), drained
1 tbsp. fresh lemon juice
1 clove garlic, chopped fine
1 tbsp. olive oil

1/2 tsp. cayenne pepper
1/2 tsp. ground cumin
1/4 tsp. dried oregano
Salt
Freshly ground pepper

Purée all ingredients in a food processor. Taste and adjust seasonings. This dip is great with toasted pita bread wedges.

Yogurt Cheese
Labaneh

Cheesecloth or coffee filters
4 cups plain yogurt (do not use
    lowfat or nonfat yogurt as
    this will result in chalky
    textured cheese)
1 tbsp. sesame seeds
1/2 tsp. salt

1/8 tsp. cayenne pepper
1/4 tsp. parsley
1/4 tsp. sage
1/4 tsp. rosemary
1/4 tsp. thyme
2 tbsps. extra-virgin olive oil
Toasted pita bread wedges

Place a fine mesh strainer over a large bowl. Line entire strainer with 3 layers of cheesecloth or with overlapping coffee filters. Spoon yogurt into lined strainer. Cover bowl and strainer with damp kitchen towel and refrigerate overnight.

In a mixing bowl, combine sesame seeds, salt and dried herbs. Transfer drained yogurt to serving bowl. Drizzle with olive oil and sprinkle with sesame seed/herb mixture. Serve with toasted pita bread wedges.

Middle Eastern Rice Jumble

1/2 yellow onion, chopped fine
2 tbsps. olive oil
2 cups white rice
4 cloves garlic, chopped fine
5 cups chicken stock
3 bay leaves
1 tbsp. freshly grated ginger

1/4 cup cider vinegar
1/2 cup pitted dates, chopped fine
1/2 cup golden raisins
1/2 cup slivered almonds
Salt
Freshly ground pepper

In a stockpot over medium-high heat, sauté onion in olive oil until golden brown. Add rice and stir until rice is lightly browned. Add remaining ingredients except almonds and bring to a boil. Reduce heat and let simmer until liquid is absorbed and rice is tender, about 20 minutes. Remove from heat and stir in almonds. Season with salt and pepper to taste.

Jack Fingersh pours wine for his guests.

Eggplant with Tahini
Baba Ghanouj

1 large eggplant
1 medium yellow onion,
   chopped fine
2 tsps. water
2 tbsps. fresh lemon juice
1 cup fresh parsley, chopped

1/2 cup tahini
1/2 tsp. cayenne pepper
3 cloves garlic, chopped fine
Salt
Freshly ground pepper

Preheat oven to 450 degrees. Bake whole, unpeeled eggplant until skin is charred and eggplant is tender, about 30 minutes. Remove and let cool. Cut eggplant in half lengthwise and scoop out pulp. Chop into 1/2-inch pieces. In a mixing bowl combine eggplant, onion, 1 tsp. lemon juice and chopped parsley. Mix well. In separate bowl, combine tahini, garlic, cayenne and remaining lemon juice. Stir in small amount of water until smooth. Fold this into the eggplant mixture. Season with salt and pepper to taste. Serve with pita bread or as a side dish.

Bulgarian Chilled Yogurt Soup
Tarato

2 tbsps. extra-virgin olive oil
1/2 yellow onion, sliced very thin
1 cup dry white wine
2 cloves garlic
3 cups plain yogurt (do not use
   lowfat or nonfat yogurt)

3 cups water
1 tbsp. cider vinegar
2 cucumbers, peeled and diced fine
Fresh dill, chopped, for garnish
Salt
Freshly ground pepper

In a heavy skillet over medium-high heat, sauté onions in oil until golden and beginning to caramelize. Add wine and garlic and bring to boil. Reduce heat and let simmer until wine is evaporated. Remove skillet from heat and let onions chill in pan. When onions are cooled stir all remaining ingredients into skillet, scraping up any browned bits of onion and garlic. Mix well and pour into serving bowl. Cover with plastic wrap and chill in refrigerator for 2-3 hours. Drizzle with extra virgin olive oil and garnish with dill before serving.

Borscht

3 tbsps. olive oil
1 large red onion, chopped fine
1 head red cabbage, shredded
 and chopped
1 bunch beets, trimmed on both
 ends, washed and diced

4 carrots, peeled and diced
4 qts. beef stock
4 tbsps. tomato paste
2 tbsps. lemon juice
2 tbsps. sugar
4 cloves garlic, chopped fine

In a stockpot over medium-high heat, sauté onion in oil until it begins to caramelize. Add cabbage, carrots and beets and cook for about 5 minutes. Add stock, tomato paste, lemon juice, sugar and garlic. Bring to a boil. Reduce heat and let simmer, uncovered, for 2 hours. Serve in soup bowls with a dollop of sour cream on top.

Pot Roast with Dates
Gedempte Fleisch

3 lbs. boneless chuck roast
2 tbsps. olive oil
5 large yellow onions, sliced thin
5 cloves garlic, chopped fine
1 tbsp. parsley, chopped fine
1 tbsp. chives, chopped fine
1 tbsp. chervil, chopped fine
1 tbsp. tarragon, chopped fine
1 tsp. cinnamon
2 cups beef stock

2 cups dry red wine
1 cup pitted dates
2 lbs. chicken legs
2 tsps. paprika
6 large carrots, halved lengthwise,
 cut into 3-inch strips
1/4 cup fresh lemon juice
1/2 cup brown sugar
Salt
Freshly ground pepper

Cut the roast into 6 to 8 pieces. Season with salt and pepper. In a wide-bottomed stockpot or Dutch oven, over medium-high heat, brown meat in olive oil. When meat is browned, remove and set aside. Reduce heat and add onions and garlic. Cook until onions are translucent. Add stock, wine, herbs and cinnamon. Return beef to pot. Bring to boil. Reduce heat and let simmer for about 1 hour.

Remove beef pieces. Add chicken legs and carrots to bottom of pot. Add dates on top of chicken and carrots. Place beef pieces on top of chicken and dates. Bring to a boil. Reduce heat and let simmer until chicken is tender, about 1 hour. Add more stock if necessary to prevent burning or drying out. Before serving stir lemon juice and brown sugar to pan juices. Each serving should include beef, chicken, dates and pan juices spooned over all.

Braised Brisket
Gahntze Tzimmes

3-4 lbs. brisket
2 tbsps. vegetable shortening
3 large carrots, peeled and cut in
   1-inch pieces
1 cup pitted prunes
1 cup dried apricots
1 lemon, sliced thin

3 large sweet potatoes, peeled
   and cut in 1-inch cubes
4 cups (or more) beef stock
1/4 cup freshly squeezed orange
   juice
1-1/2 tbsps. brown sugar
2 tbsps. flour

Preheat oven to 400 degrees. In a heavy skillet over high heat, brown brisket in shortening. Transfer brisket to a roasting pan. Place carrots and sweet potatoes around edge of meat. Layer prunes, apricots and lemon slices on top of brisket. Combine stock, orange juice and brown sugar and bring to a boil. Pour over brisket. If necessary, add additional stock up to the top of the brisket. Cover and roast for 1 hour. After 1 hour reduce heat to 325 degrees and continue roasting for 4-1/2 hours. Uncover and roast for another 30 minutes.

Cholent
This dish is traditionally prepared on Friday for Saturday so as not to violate Jewish laws regarding work on the Sabbath. Like Kansas City barbecue, this dish actually benefits from a long, slow cooking process.

3 lbs. brisket
2 cups dried lima beans
3 yellow onions, chopped fine
2 tsps. paprika
1/4 tsp. pepper
1/4 tsp. ginger
2 tbsps. flour

6 to 8 potatoes, peeled
1 cup pearled barley
8-12 eggs
2 tsps. salt
2 tbsps. olive oil
2 to 3 quarts boiling water

Preheat oven to 250 degrees. Soak lima beans in water overnight. Drain and rinse. In a heavy, wide-bottomed stockpot brown brisket and onions in olive oil. Season with salt, pepper and ginger. Add beans, barley and potatoes to pot. Sprinkle with flour and paprika. Carefully place uncooked eggs in pot. Add enough boiling water to cover — to at least 1 inch above — brisket, beans, potatoes and eggs. Cover. Cook for 24 hours.

Orange Curry Chicken

3 lbs. chicken pieces
4 tbsps. butter
1/2 cup brown sugar
1/2 cup undiluted orange juice
    concentrate

1/4 cup whole-grain mustard
3 cloves garlic, chopped fine
1 tbsp. curry powder
1 tsp. salt

Preheat oven to 375 degrees. In a small saucepan, melt butter over medium heat. Stir in brown sugar, orange juice concentrate, mustard, garlic, curry powder and salt. Arrange chicken in baking dish and cover with sauce. Bake for 1 hour.

Marinated Lamb Kebabs
Shishlik

3 lbs. lamb, cut in 1-inch cubes
6 cloves garlic, crushed
6 tbsps. extra-virgin olive oil
2 tbsps. sugar
1/2 cup vinegar

3 bay leaves
2 tsps. cayenne pepper
2 tbsps. salt
1 tbsp. freshly ground pepper

Combine all ingredients, except lamb, in an airtight plastic container. Mix well. Add lamb pieces and stir to coat well. Cover and marinate overnight or at least 8 hours.

Soak bamboo skewers in water for 30 minutes prior to grilling. At the same time soak several chunks of apple or cherry wood in water.

Start a charcoal fire in a wood/charcoal burning kettle-type grill such as a Weber. Use natural lump charcoal. Do not use lighter fluid. Start the fire with a paraffin starter stick. When charcoal is covered in a fine gray ash, put grill rack in. Skewer lamb cubes. Sprinkle with salt and pepper. Grill until lamb is still just slightly pink in the middle.

Ring Bologna and Sauerkraut

1 lb. ring bologna, sliced thin
    (casing removed if necessary)
1 red onion, sliced thin
2 tbsps. vegetable oil

2 lbs. sauerkraut, with liquid
1 (15 oz.) can diced tomatoes,
    with liquid
1/2 cup brown sugar

In a heavy skillet, over medium-high heat, sauté bologna and onions in vegetable oil until they begin to brown. Remove from heat. In a large saucepan, combine bologna, onions, sauerkraut, tomatoes and sugar. Bring to a boil. Cover, reduce heat and let simmer for 30 minutes or more.

Sephardic Meat Pies
Burekas

For the pastry:
2 sticks butter, chilled, cut in
   small pieces
2 tsps. salt

6 cups self-rising flour
Warm water
2 egg yolks
4 tbsps. sesame seeds

In a large mixing bowl, working quickly, use fingertips to knead butter pieces into flour until mixture is the consistency of coarse crumbs. Add just enough warm water to make a smooth, stiff dough. On a lightly floured work surface, roll dough into a sheet about 1/8-inch thick. Using a cup or a cookie cutter, cut into disks.

For the filling:
1 cup feta cheese
2 cup chopped spinach, cooked
1 tsp. dill
2 cloves garlic, chopped fine

1 tbsp. lemon zest
6 egg yolks
Salt
Freshly ground pepper

Preheat oven to 350 degrees. In a large mixing bowl, combine all ingredients and mix well. Put 1 tablespoon of filling on each pastry disk. Fold in half and seal by pressing edges with tines of fork. Brush each bureka with beaten egg yolks. Then sprinkle with sesame seeds. Arrange pies on greased cookie sheet and bake about 15-20 minutes, until golden-brown. Serve warm.

Seared Salmon with Hummus and Sesame Seed Crust

4 (8 oz.) salmon fillets, skin on,
   small bones and excess fat
   removed
2 cups hummus (see recipe,
   Page 160)

2 cups sesame seeds
4 tbsps. canola (or sesame seed) oil

Preheat oven to 400 degrees.

Using your hand, a rubber spatula or the back of a spoon, spread about 1/2 cup of hummus on the skin side of each fillet. Sprinkle about 1/2 cup of sesame seeds evenly over the hummus. Press the seeds into the hummus.

In a large, heavy ovenproof skillet over high heat, sear the bottom of each fillet (hummus side up), about 3-4 minutes. Transfer skillet to oven and bake for about 30 minutes. Garnish with cilantro and lemon wedges.

Esther about to enjoy her daughter's dessert.

Eggs in Tomato Sauce
Shakshouka

1 yellow onion, chopped fine
3 tbsps. olive oil
6 ripe tomatoes, seeded and diced
2 cloves garlic, chopped fine

4 slices of roasted red pepper
   (bottled), chopped
4 eggs
Salt
Freshly ground pepper

In a heavy skillet over medium-high heat, sauté onion until lightly browned. Add tomatoes, peppers and garlic. Cover and simmer over low heat for about 30 minutes.

Uncover and stir. Break eggs directly into sauce. Break yolks and stir gently once or twice. Cover and cook for about 3-4 minutes, or until eggs are set. Season with salt and pepper.

Carla and Tiberius Klausner.

Cheese Blintzes

For the filling:
1-1/2 cups dry cottage cheese
1 (8 oz.) package cream cheese
1 egg, slightly beaten

2 tsps. cinnamon
3 tbsps. sugar
1/2 cup pitted prunes, chopped

In a mixing bowl, combine cheeses, cinnamon, sugar and egg. Mix well. Fold in prunes.

For the batter:
1 cup flour
1 cup whole milk
1/4 tsp. salt

2 eggs
Vegetable shortening
(for cooking)

Preheat oven to 350 degrees. In a mixing bowl, combine flour, milk and salt. Add eggs and beat until smooth. Heat a small skillet to medium high. (If a drop of water "dances" when dropped onto the skillet, it's ready. If it sizzles and disappears, it's too hot.) Add enough vegetable shortening to grease cooking surface. Spoon just enough batter into the skillet to coat bottom — tipping the skillet to spread batter thin. Do not flip as you would a pancake. Cook on one side only, then turn blintzes onto a paper towel. Spoon approximately 1-1/2 tablespoons of filling in a line from one edge of the blintz to the other and roll up jellyroll-style. Arrange on a baking sheet and bake for 10 minutes.

Cheese Balls

1 cup dry cottage cheese
2 eggs, separated
2 tbsps. sugar

1/2 tsp. salt
1/2 cup, or more, matzo meal
2 tbsps. butter, melted

In a mixing bowl, beat egg whites until stiff. In a separate bowl, mix cheese, egg yolks, sugar and salt. Gradually stir in enough matzo meal to make a thick batter. Add butter and stir. Then gently fold in egg whites. Cover and chill for 30 minutes.

Start a pot of water boiling. Scoop out about a tablespoon at a time of batter and roll between your palms to make small balls. Carefully drop balls into boiling water. When they rise to the top scoop them out with a slotted spoon and let cool on waxed paper. May be served with applesauce, sprinkled with cinnamon-sugar, or with sour cream on top.

Caramel Oranges

4-6 large ripe navel oranges	3/4 cup heavy cream
1 cup sugar	3 tbsps. orange liqueur
1 tsp. cinnamon	1 tsp. fresh lemon juice
1/2 tsp. cloves	2 tsps. cider vinegar

Peel and slice oranges into rounds. You might get 3 good-sized slices per orange. Carefully remove all white pith around the edge of each slice. Arrange on the bottom of a glass serving dish.

In a heavy saucepan cook the sugar, cinnamon and cloves over medium-low heat, stirring constantly with a whisk, until melted and lightly caramel-colored. Cook, without stirring, by swirling pan, until deep golden. Remove pan from heat. In a small mixing bowl combine cream, liqueur, lemon juice and vinegar. Slowly and carefully stir in cream mixture. Caramel will start to harden during this process. Return pan to heat and simmer, until the caramel is dissolved. Pour over oranges. Serve warm as a dessert.

Noodle Pudding
Kugel

1 (12 oz.) package wide egg noodles	1-1/4 cups sugar
2 sticks butter, melted	8 eggs, beaten
1 lb. ricotta cheese	2 cups milk
1 cup sour cream	1/2 tsp. vanilla extract
1 (8 oz.) package cream cheese, softened	1/2 cup golden raisins
	1/2 cup dried apricots, diced
	2 tsps. cinnamon

Preheat oven to 350 degrees. Cook noodles until tender in boiling salted water and drain. In a large mixing bowl, combine noodles with butter, cheese, sour cream and sugar. Mix thoroughly. Spoon noodle mixture into a 9-by-13 baking dish and spread evenly. In another mixing bowl, combine egg, milk, vanilla, raisins and apricots. Mix well and pour over noodle mixture. Bake for 1 hour.

Italian Traditions

"Americans eat to live.
Italians live to eat."

Joe Avelluto Sr. is my own personal Cupid. If it weren't for his tomato and cucumber salad and his prosciutto balls, my wife and I might never have fallen in love. And God knows what my life would be like without her.

It was at Italian Delight, Joe's little Johnson County café, that we first had lunch together. We liked each other enough — and Joe's food enough — that we went back. Many times. And always we ordered the same salad and three prosciutto balls each, with a little extra red sauce on the side. Eventually our casual lunchtime conversations turned to deeper discussions of our lives, losses and hopes. Approximately 124 prosciutto balls later, we were in love.

Though Joe Avelluto's restaurant has an unassuming, old-suburb charm, no one, not even Joe, would necessarily call it romantic. The cafeteria-style eatery is a clean, well-lighted place, anchoring the corner of an aging strip mall. It doesn't look like the kind of place you'd find romance. But when you eat at Italian Delight be prepared to be delighted.

Since 1983, when Joe and his wife, Rose, first opened the

Left: Joe Avelutto Sr. makes fresh mozzarella. Above: Joe's grandson Dominic.

restaurant, Italian Delight has been serving some of the Kansas City area's best, most authentic Italian food. Nothing fancy. Nothing pretentious. Just really good food. And because Joe and his family are the ones who actually cook the food and put it on your plate, once you become a regular at Italian Delight, you're treated like family. And the place becomes, well, *your* place. And there is something kind of romantic about that.

Joe Avelluto was 22 years old when he first came to the United States from Mola Di Bari, Italy, in 1962 as an exchange student. A couple years later he met and married Rose Laudadio in New York City and there they started their family. They had four sons: John, Joe Jr., James and Michael. The Y-chromosome is clearly dominant in the Avelluto family. The oldest three boys are now married and their unions have produced

The Avelluto family's roots extend deep into Puglia, the "heel" of the boot-shaped Italian peninsula. It is the easternmost region of Italy and is characterized by its hot, dry weather and its long, scenic coastline.

Approximately two-thirds of the olive oil produced in Italy comes from Puglia. It should be no surprise then that olive oil is so fundamental to Pugliese cooking. Puglia also leads all other regions of Italy in grape production.

The climate in Puglia is ideal for growing many fruits and vegetables — including tomatoes, eggplant, fennel, peppers, cauliflower, broccoli, lettuces, chicory and onions — and these are important in the regional cuisine.

Puglia boasts that the best durum wheat in the world is grown in its fields. It is natural therefore that pasta would form the foundation of the region's cuisine.

Because it is surrounded by ocean, seafood is obviously an integral part of Pugliese cooking. Beef was introduced into the local diet only within the last 100 years.

Though Pugliese food is a cornerstone of Italian cuisine it has itself been significantly influenced by Greek cooking traditions, as may be seen in the prevalence of olives, spinach, lemon, garlic and lamb — among other foods — in the local diet.

five grandsons for Joe and Rose.

All the grandsons are present, accounted for and chasing each other around when I join the family for a late lunch at Italian Delight. John's wife, Patti, is mostly successful in keeping her energetic sons Dominic and Gianni corralled while waiting for Grandpa to emerge from the kitchen with the eats. Joe Jr.'s wife, Metissa, holds their 2-year-old, Massimo, on her lap while she chats with James' wife, Melissa, who is gently bouncing her baby, Rocco, on her knee. Her No.1 son, Anthony, is talking with his dad, who has just pulled a pizza from the oven and is cutting it for a customer.

This has been a family business right from the start, explains Joe Sr. "All the boys have worked here since they were kids. I think it's been mostly good for them. Maybe sometimes they'd rather be doing something else. But now that they're older I think they're proud of what we do. My father, Giovanni Avelluto, was a chef and my brother, Dominick, is a restaurateur in New York City. So I guess this business is in our blood."

Italian Delight started as a New York-style pizza parlor. "We'd been here in Kansas City, in the restaurant business, for about six years when we got the idea that this part of town could use a good pizza place," says Joe Sr. "We were confident that our style of pizza and our quality would attract customers."

And so they did. Soon Joe was adding other traditional Italian items to the menu.

"We wanted to provide our customers with the taste of *authentic* Italian food," Joe says. "Most people are used to an Americanized version."

Word got out and the little storefront joint became a favorite of foodies and aficionados. Newspaper columnists and critics praised the restaurant's combination of genuine, yet affordable, Italian cuisine and homey, quirky character.

"If you give people an honest product, they will appreciate it," Joe states.

Several years ago, eldest son John and his brother Joe Jr. struck out on their own with Il Trullo, an upscale Italian restaurant in Overland

Rose Avelluto brings a platter of bruschetta to the table.

Joe Avelluto explains how it is.

Park, Kansas. Il Trullo specializes in the cuisine of Puglia, the region of Italy from which the Avelluto family came.

"The restaurant business is hard," John admits. "It's hard on your family life. And it's exhausting. But it's also about the most rewarding business there is. It's so fundamental. I mean, you're *feeding* people. That's about as basic as it gets. But when you do a good job of it, people are grateful and that's very satisfying."

When I ask him what it's like working day in and day out with members of your own family, he rolls his eyes. "You have to get real good at lettin' things go in one ear and out the other. Otherwise you'll go nuts."

Twice identified by *USA Today* as the Italian restaurant worth seeking out when traveling to Kansas City, Il Trullo has established itself

as a dining destination. John says that he and his brother Joe are doing their best to carry forward their father's commitment to authenticity.

"We've traveled extensively around Puglia, in Italy, to research recipes and to bring back dishes that reflect the food traditions there," he says.

John observes that the attitude toward food is quite different in Italy compared to here in the United States. "Food is everything in Italian culture. Americans eat to live. Italians live to eat. No matter what your economic status is, in Italy you find a way to buy good food."

Even the buying of the food is different in Italy.

"There you shop each day for the things you'll need *that day*," John says. "In most Italian towns and cities there are no American-style supermarkets where you can buy everything all at once. You still have to go to individual shops to buy each of your food items separately. And you end up developing relationships with your butcher, your produce man, your dry goods man, your baker. And these relationships become extremely important for both you and the shop owners. You count on them for fresh, quality food. Every day. And they count on you for their livelihood. Here in America it's all mostly anonymous. Nobody here knows who cuts their meat."

Joe Avelluto Sr. arrives at the table with a platter of brilliant green asparagus topped with thin slices of Parmesan cheese in one hand and a plateful of green beans and diced tomatoes glistening with olive oil in the other. His sons and daughters-in-law waste no time in filling their plates. Joe Jr. laughs. "You can see how passionate we are about our food," he says.

There was a time, however, when it appeared that Joe Jr. might chart a course away from the family enterprise. After graduating from the University of Kansas, he left home to attend law school in New York City. To help pay for his education Joe Jr. worked at his uncle's restaurant where his interest in food and wine matured. He quit law school, moved back to Kansas City and joined his father and brothers in the business.

He shrugs his shoulders. "I tried to get out. But the food is just too good."

At the other end of the table, John is sampling a new variety of olives his father has just brought. "Hey, Joe! Try these," he motions.

"We've gotta start serving these at the restaurant." Joe stuffs a few in his mouth and nods in agreement.

Also on the table is a bruschetta with a rich, almost-purple tapenade; an antipasto of mozzarella and olives; a salad of tomatoes, basil and mozzarella; and freshly ground pepper.

Then the patriarch brings in the main dish — a ragout of veal, pork and beef rolled around prosciutto slices, stewed in a spicy homemade tomato sauce. The children, who haven't much cared for the appetizers and salads, quickly line up, plates in hand, for helpings of this delicious family specialty.

Rose Avelluto smiles. "I like to see the little ones eat," she says.

Rose explains that because the family's restaurants are open so many hours of the week, it's hard for her clan to get together for family meals. "My boys are so busy feeding other people that I never get a chance to feed them myself," she sighs.

Joe and Rose's youngest son, Michael, is a senior in high school and thinks maybe he'll study information technology in college. Or maybe not. He's still young. He's got time to decide what to do with his life. If he follows the path his father took, he'll try several things before he arrives at his final destination. Before opening his first restaurant in 1977, Joe Sr. was a cabinetmaker, a printer in a textile factory and, for 10 years, a longshoreman in Brooklyn, New York.

"I've learned a lot from my dad," says Michael. "He's taught me to be generous and to love my family. And he's also shown me how to work hard, to be innovative and to try new things."

"I've never been afraid to take risks," Joe says. "If you don't take risks you get stale. And, just like food, if you get stale you aren't good for much.

"Authenticity. That's the key. It's got to be real. Whatever you do, whatever business you're in. And you have to truly love it. For me it's food. And I do love it."

I tell Joe about falling in love with my wife right here in his restaurant. He smiles and squeezes my shoulder. "Well, I'm glad we could provide you with that service," he says. "And, see, it's like I told you. It's all about love."

Avelluto Family Recipes
and other traditional Italian dishes

Avelluto's Tomato Sauce

2 lbs. fresh plum tomatoes
1/2 yellow onion, chopped fine
2 medium carrots, chopped fine
1/2 cup fresh parsley, chopped
2 stalks celery, chopped fine,
including leaves

5 fresh basil leaves, roughly
chopped
1/4 cup extra-virgin olive oil
Salt
Freshly ground pepper

Wash and dice tomatoes. In a heavy saucepan, combine tomatoes with olive oil, onions, carrots, parsley, celery and basil. Cover and cook over low heat for about 30 minutes, stirring occasionally. Uncover and further reduce until sauce is no longer watery. Add salt and pepper to taste.

Anthony Avelluto.

Raw Tomato Sauce

12 ripe plum tomatoes
5 tbsps. extra-virgin olive oil
1/2 cup fresh basil, chopped fine

4 cloves garlic, chopped fine
Salt
Freshly ground pepper

Wash tomatoes well and cut each into about 6 wedges. Remove seeds. In a mixing bowl, toss tomatoes with olive oil, basil, garlic and salt and pepper to taste. This is great as salad by itself and even better served with cold pasta.

Joe spoons some penne onto a grandson's plate. That's Rocco Avelluto on the right.

Pizzaiola Tomato Sauce

2 lbs. fresh plum tomatoes, or
   2 (16 oz.) cans Italian plum
   tomatoes
1/2 cup extra-virgin olive oil
2 cloves garlic, chopped fine

1/2 cup fresh oregano, chopped
1/2 cup fresh parsley, chopped
Salt
Freshly ground pepper

Wash tomatoes well and cut each into about 6 wedges. Remove seeds and cut wedges into fine dice. In a heavy saucepan sauté garlic in olive oil until golden brown. Add tomatoes, salt and pepper to taste and cook over high heat. When the tomatoes are cooked down to a thick sauce add the oregano and parsley and cook for a few more minutes. This sauce nicely complements meats.

Arrabbiata Spicy Tomato Sauce

2 lbs. fresh plum tomatoes, or
   2 (16 oz.) cans Italian plum
   tomatoes
1/4 cup extra-virgin olive oil
2 cloves garlic, chopped fine

2-3 pepperocini (hot peppers),
   diced
1/2 cup fresh parsley, chopped
Salt
Freshly ground pepper

Wash tomatoes well and cut each into about 6 wedges. Remove seeds and cut wedges into fine dice. In a heavy saucepan sauté garlic and hot peppers in olive oil. Add tomatoes, salt and pepper to taste and cook over high heat. When the tomatoes are cooked down to a thick sauce add the parsley and cook for a few more minutes.

Ragout Tomato Sauce

2 lbs. stewing meat (may be beef, pork, or veal), cubed
1/2 cup extra-virgin olive oil
1 tbsp. lard
4 slices prosciutto, cut in thin strips
2 lbs. fresh plum tomatoes, or 2 (16 oz.) cans Italian plum tomatoes

1 cup dry red wine
1 yellow onion, chopped fine
2 cloves garlic, chopped fine
2 medium carrots, chopped fine
2 stalks celery, chopped fine, including leaves
1/2 cup fresh parsley, chopped
Salt
Freshly ground pepper

In a heavy saucepan over medium-high heat, sauté stewing meat and onions in lard until onion begins to caramelize. Add prosciutto, garlic and red wine. When meat is well browned and the wine is reduced to about one-third its original volume add the tomatoes. Cover and reduce heat. After 15 minutes add celery, carrots and parsley. Bring back to a boil, reduce heat and let simmer for about 2 hours. This rich sauce is good for pasta dishes, risotto or timballi.

Rigatoni Alla Vodka

Joe Avelluto recommends using fresh, not dry, pasta whenever possible.

16 oz. rigatoni
4 shallots, chopped fine
1/2 stick butter
2 bay leaves
Hot pepper flakes to taste
1 cup heavy cream

3 cups bottled marinara sauce or Avelluto's tomato sauce
2 cups freshly grated Parmesan reggiano
Splash of vodka

Cook rigatoni *al dente* in boiling salted water. Rinse in cold water, drain and set aside. In heavy skillet, sauté shallots in butter until golden. Add bay leaf, pepper, cream and vodka. Bring to a boil. Add marinara sauce and Parmesan cheese. Stir the rigatoni into the sauce and serve.

Spaghetti Aglio E Olio

10-12 oz. spaghetti
6-8 tbsps. extra virgin olive oil
4 cloves garlic, chopped fine

1 tsp. red pepper flakes
Salt

Cook spaghetti al dente in boiling salted water. Rinse in cold water, drain and set aside. In a heavy skillet sauté garlic in oil with pepper flakes and salt to taste. When garlic begins to brown stir in spaghetti. Toss and serve immediately.

Pizza Margherita

For dough:
2-3/4 cups bread flour	1 tsp. sugar
1 tsp. salt	3/4 cup warm water
1 tsp. active dried yeast	1 tbsp. extra virgin olive oil

For topping:
	1/2 cup fresh basil, chopped
8 oz. fresh mozzarella, sliced thin	8 fresh plum tomatoes, peeled,
4 tbsps. extra-virgin olive oil	seeded and diced

In a small bowl, combine yeast, sugar and 1/4 cup water. Let sit until frothy. Add yeast liquid to flour with remaining water and oil. Mix to a soft dough; knead on a floured surface 10 minutes until smooth. Place in a greased bowl; cover with plastic wrap. Let rise in a warm place 45 minutes or until doubled in size. Punch down dough and knead briefly. Oil a 12-inch pizza pan.

Transfer to a well floured work table. Cut in dough in 4 equal parts and stretch into 4 round little pizza disks.

Top each with fresh mozzarella and tomatoes. Then add fresh basil and salt and pepper to taste. Drizzle with 3 tbsp. of olive oil. Put in preheated oven at 600 degrees. Cook for 8 minutes. When pizzas are ready, drizzle with another tablespoon of olive oil, and serve.

Spaghetti Alla Puttanesca

1/2 lb. spaghetti	1 tsp. oregano
4 tbsps. extra-virgin olive oil	1 tsp. freshly ground pepper
2 cloves garlic, chopped fine	12 black olives
2 shallots, chopped fine	20 capers
1 tsp. red pepper flakes	12 oz. marinara sauce
6 anchovies, chopped	

Cook spaghetti al dente in boiling salted water. Rinse in cold water, drain and set aside. In a heavy skillet sauté garlic and shallots in oil with pepper flakes and salt to taste. When garlic begins to brown add anchovies, olives, capers, oregano and marinara sauce and bring to a boil. Reduce heat and let simmer for 3-4 minutes. Add spaghetti to skillet. Toss and serve immediately.

Linguini Alla Vongole

16 oz. linguini
4 cloves garlic, chopped fine
1-1/2 sticks butter
1 cup fresh parsley, chopped

Dash white pepper
Salt to taste
8-12 clams, minced
1 cup clam juice

Cook linguini *al dente* in boiling salted water. Rinse in cold water, drain and set aside. In a heavy skillet, sauté garlic in butter until just beginning to turn golden. Do not burn. Add clams and clam juice and bring to a boil. Reduce heat and let simmer uncovered until clams are tender and liquid is reduced by one-third. Stir linguini into sauce and mix well. Serve immediately.

Lasagna Nostra

1-1/2 lbs. of lasagna pasta
2 cups tomato sauce
1 lb. lean ground beef
3 cloves garlic, chopped fine
1/2 yellow onion, chopped fine
3/4 lb. ricotta cheese

1/2 lb. mozzarella cheese, grated
1 to 1-1/2 cups freshly grated
   Parmesan cheese
Salt
Freshly ground pepper to taste

Cook the lasagna *al dente* in boiling salted water. Drain and spread noodles flat on table or counter to dry.

Preheat oven to 400 degrees.

In a heavy skillet, cook ground beef, garlic and onion over medium-high heat until meat in completely browned and crumbly.

Cover bottom of a 9-by-9 baking dish with about 2/3 cup tomato sauce, seasoned to taste with salt and pepper. Cover with two layers of lasagna. Add a layer of crumbled ricotta cheese, grated mozzarella, ground beef, another 2/3 cup tomato sauce and half of the Parmesan cheese. Add another layer of lasagna. Repeat layer of cheeses, meat, tomato sauce and Parmesan. Bake for 30 minutes at 400 degrees.

James Avelluto. James pretty much runs things at Italian Delight.

Seafood Soup
Il Trullo's Zuppa Dimare

1/2 cup extra-virgin olive oil
6 cloves fresh garlic, crushed
1 tsp. red pepper flakes
12 littleneck clams, cleaned,
   scrubbed and debearded
3 (15 oz.) cans crushed tomatoes
3 cups fish or chicken stock
3/4 cup roughly chopped Italian or
   curly leaf parsley

1/3 lb. (6 oz.) calamari, cleaned
   and cut into pieces, including
   tentacles and body
12 shrimp, peeled and de-veined
1/2 lb. (8 oz.) monkfish (salmon,
   tuna or sea bass may be
   substituted) cut into 2-inch
   chunks

In a large stockpot over medium heat sauté garlic and pepper flakes in olive oil. Add the clams. When the garlic starts to brown add tomatoes. Bring mixture to a boil. Add half the stock and half the parsley and reduce heat to medium. Add monkfish, calamari and shrimp and cook until shrimp turns pink. Garnish with remaining parsley.

This dish may be served with or without pasta or rice. If you have some day-old bread, toast it and put it on the bottom of the soup bowl before you ladle in the soup.

Tagliatelle
Three "Ps:" Peas, Prosciutto and Parmesan

1/2 lb. *tagliatelle* pasta
2 tbsp. butter
1 cup frozen peas, thawed
6 slices prosciutto, diced

1 tsp. red pepper flakes
2 cups heavy cream
1 cup freshly grated Parmesan
   cheese

Cook tagliatelle *al dente* in boiling salted water. Rinse in cold water, drain and set aside. In a heavy skillet sauté prosciutto in butter. Add peas, cook for 3 minutes. Add cream, pepper flakes and grated Parmesan bring to a boil. Stir in tagliatelle, mix thoroughly and serve immediately.

Orecchiette ("Little Ears") con Broccoli di Rapa

1 lb. orecchiette (pasta shaped like "little ears"; any small pasta will do)
1/2 cup extra-virgin olive oil
2 cloves garlic, sliced very thin

6 anchovy fillets, boned and coarsely chopped
1/2 tsp. red pepper flakes
1 lb. (2 bunches) broccoli-rape
Salt
Freshly ground pepper

In a saucepan sauté garlic over medium heat. When garlic begins to soften and turn golden add the anchovies. Continue to cook over medium-low heat, crushing the anchovy fillets with the back of a fork, making a coarse paste. Add pepper flakes. Mix well and set aside.

Wash the broccoli-rape, discarding any yellow or tough outer leaves and trimming the thick stems. Coarsely chop the leaves, leaving any little flower clusters intact.

Bring large pot of lightly salted water to a boil and add broccoli-rape. Boil, uncovered, for about 3 minutes. Add the orecchiette to the water and boil for another 10 minutes. Drain pasta in a colander and transfer to a warm bowl. Add the anchovy-garlic sauce and toss to mix well. Taste and add salt if necessary (the anchovies may give it sufficient salt). Add lots of black pepper. Serve immediately.

Gnocchi

Gnocchi are delicious little dumplings usually made with potatoes and flour.
This is how Joe Avelluto says he makes them.

"The ratio of potato to flour can vary from one region to another, depending on local Italian customs and traditions, as well as on the kind of potatoes used. Gnocchi may also be made with flour, semolina, ricotta, spinach or bread crumbs. Gnocchetti are smaller than gnocchi. Here in the United States, Idaho potatoes are the most suitable for gnocchi. Do not use early potatoes, as they are typically too watery.

"Wash about 1 pound of Idaho baking potatoes. Place them unpeeled in a large pot of cold, lightly salted water. Bring to a boil. Cooking time will vary depending on potato type and size. Cook until fork tender. Remove from water and let cool.

"Peel potatoes using a paring knife. In a large mixing bowl mash potatoes using a potato ricer. If the puree is too watery, spoon it into a sauce pan and, over moderate heat, stir the mixture to let it dry. It is important that the potato puree be dry. Otherwise too much flour will have to be used in the mix and the gnocchi will turn become doughy and heavy.

"Add a pinch of salt as you mash the potatoes, then gradually add flour to make a soft dough. Add only enough that dough no longer sticks to your fingers. The dough should not be kneaded too much, only long enough to blend the potatoes and flour.

"Roll a piece of the dough into a long cylinder about the thickness of your index finger. Cut this cylinder into 1-inch pieces. Repeat this process until the dough is used up.

"Gnocchi should not be prepared too far in advance of cooking. Drop finished gnocchi into a large pot of boiling lightly salted water. Cook until gnocchi float to the top, usually about 3-5. Then lift them out of water with a skimmer or a slotted spoon. Do not drain in a colander. Place gnocchi in a warm bowl. Toss with Avelluto's tomato sauce, a puttanesca sauce, or drizzle with extra-virgin olive oil and sprinkle with freshly grated Parmesan. Serve immediately."

Fettuccine Alfredo

This Italian classic is typically prepared at the last possible moment before serving, so it's best to have all your ingredients ready to go.

1 lb. fettuccine	1 cup freshly grated Parmesan
2 cups heavy cream	Freshly ground pepper

Cook the fettuccine *al dente* in heavily salted boiling water. Have ready a large skillet heated to medium high. Drain pasta and pour into skillet with a few tablespoons of the cooking water. Add heavy cream and grated Parmesan. Stir to combine well. The result should be a smooth, velvety sauce. Add freshly ground pepper and serve immediately.

Simple Tiramisu

3 eggs yolks	1/4 cup brandy
6 tbsps. sugar	3 dozen ladyfingers
1-1/2 cups mascarpone (Italian cream cheese)	2 tbsps. cocoa powder
	1/4 cup crushed amaretto biscuits
1 cup strong coffee or espresso	

In a stainless steel mixing bowl held over a saucepan of simmering water, whisk the egg yolks with the sugar until pale yellow ribbons fall from the whisk. Add the brandy and continue to whisk gently. Remove from heat and let cool.

Add the mascarpone and half the espresso and continue to whisk until mixture is smooth. Moisten the ladyfingers with the remaining espresso. Line the bottom of a deep glass dessert dish with ladyfingers. Cover with mascarpone mixture. Add another layer of ladyfingers and then another layer of mascarpone. Finally one more layer of ladyfingers and then a final layer of mascarpone. Refrigerate for about 2 hours. Just before serving, mix 2 tbsps. cocoa powder with crushed amaretto biscuits and sprinkle evenly over the top.

The following are not Avelluto family recipes but are typical folk foods of the Puglia and Campania regions of Italy.

Apulian Tomato Salad

4 large ripe tomatoes
2 tbsps. fresh parsley, chopped
2 tbsps. fresh chives, chopped
2 tbsps. fresh basil
2 tbsps. fresh mint
2 tbsps. bread crumbs

1/4 cup freshly grated
   Pecorino-Romano cheese
3 tbsps. extra virgin olive oil
Salt
Freshly ground pepper
3 tbsps. extra-virgin olive oil

Preheat oven to 350 degrees.

Remove the seeds from the tomato slices. Salt on both sides and lay slices in single layer in a colander. After 15 minutes rinse tomatoes and dry with paper towel. Arrange slices on the bottom of a well-greased baking dish. In a mixing bowl, combine parsley, chives, basil, mint, breadcrumbs, Romano and salt and pepper. Sprinkle this mixture over the tomatoes, drizzle with oil and bake about 20 minutes.

Rebecca's Bruschetta

6 1-inch-thick slices of Italian
   bread cut diagonally
1/2 cup butter, melted
1/2 cup extra virgin olive oil
2 cloves garlic, peeled and halved
   lengthwise

3-4 ripe tomatoes, sliced very thin
8-12 leaves fresh basil, chopped
16 oz. fresh mozzarella cheese,
   cut in 1/8-inch-thick slices
Salt
Freshly ground pepper

Arrange bread slices on broiler pan or on top of cookie sheet. Combine olive oil and melted butter and brush this mixture on bread, all the way to the edges of each slice. Be careful not to let bread get soggy. Season with a little salt. Toast immediately under broiler until golden brown. Remove and let cool slightly. Rub garlic cloves on toasted bread. Top with slices of mozzarella, chopped basil, tomato slices and freshly ground pepper. Put back under the broiler and toast until cheese is bubbly and tomatoes begin to brown.

Gianni Avelluto watches his grandfather make fresh mozzarella cheese, an indispensable ingredient in Italian cooking.

Turnip Tops

3 lbs. turnip greens	1 cup dry red wine
2 cloves garlic, chopped fine	1/4 extra virgin olive oil
1/2 red onion sliced thin	Salt
2 bay leaves	Freshly ground pepper

Thoroughly wash and drain greens. In a heavy skillet sauté greens without water or oil over medium heat until limp. After about 30 minutes, reduce heat and add salt, pepper, garlic, oil, wine and bay leaves. Stir and bring to a boil. Reduce heat and let simmer over low heat for about 15 minutes. Remove bay leaves. Serve immediately.

Tomato and Bean Soup with Conchiglie "Little Shells"

8-10 ripe plum tomatoes, seeded and chopped	1/2 tsp. hot pepper flakes
Extra-virgin olive oil	1/2 tsp. dried oregano
4 cloves garlic, chopped fine	Salt
1/4 yellow onion, chopped fine	Freshly ground pepper
4 cups chicken stock	1 cup *conchiglie* ("little shells" pasta)
1 (15 oz.) can white kidney beans	Fresh grated Pecorino-Romano
1 tbsp. fresh rosemary leaves	cheese

In a stockpot, sauté the onion in olive oil over medium-high heat until caramelized. Add tomatoes, garlic, pepper flakes, oregano and rosemary. Cook for about 10 minutes. Add chicken stock and beans. Bring to a boil. Reduce heat and simmer. Season with salt and pepper.

Separately, cook 1 cup *conchiglie* in boiling salted water until al dente, just tender. Stir cooked pasta into soup. Ladle into bowls and top with fresh grated Pecorino-Romano cheese.

Ziti with Chickpeas and Olives

1 lb. ziti	8-10 green onions, cut in 3-inch lengths
1/4 cup extra virgin olive oil	1 tsp. marjoram
6 cloves garlic, cut in half lengthwise	1 cup dry white wine
1 cup canned chickpeas, drained	Salt
1 cup small black olives	Freshly ground pepper

Cook ziti *al dente* in boiling salted water. Rinse in cold water, drain and set aside. In a heavy skillet, sauté garlic in olive oil until just beginning to brown. Do not burn. Add chickpeas, olives, onions, marjoram and wine. Bring to a boil. Reduce heat and let simmer until wine is reduced to about 1/3 cup. Season with salt and pepper to taste. Stir in ziti and let simmer for a couple of minutes. Serve immediately.

Meatball and Turnip Greens Soup

For the meatballs:
1 lb. ground pork
1 cup breadcrumbs
1 egg slightly beaten
3 cloves garlic, chopped fine
1/4 cup chopped fresh parsley

For the soup:
8 cups chicken stock
1 cup dry white wine
3 cloves garlic
1/2 yellow onion, chopped fine
2 tbsps. extra virgin olive oil
2 leaves fresh sage, chopped

1/2 tsp. dried sage
1/2 tsp. dried rosemary
1/2 tsp. dried thyme
Salt
Freshly ground pepper
1 tbsp. extra virgin olive oil

1 bunch turnip greens, scrubbed,
   stemmed and very coarsely
   chopped (or not at all)
1 tsp. sugar
Salt
Freshly ground pepper
Freshly grated Parmesan

In a large mixing bowl, combine ground pork, breadcrumbs, egg, garlic and seasonings. Mix well with wooden spoon or by hand. Form small meatballs, an inch or less in diameter, from this mixture. In a heavy skillet, cook the meatballs in olive oil over medium heat for about 15 minutes, or until cooked through.

Meanwhile, in a stockpot, sauté onion in olive oil over medium-high heat until caramelized. Add wine and bring to a boil. Reduce heat and let simmer until wine is reduced to about 1/4 cup. Add chicken stock, garlic, sugar, sage and salt and pepper to taste and bring back to a boil. Reduce heat and let simmer for 10 minutes or so. Add turnip greens and bring back to a boil. Reduce heat and let simmer until greens are entirely cooked and tender. Add meatballs and let simmer another 5-10 minutes. Serve in bowls with freshly grated Parmesan on top.

Fava Puree with Chicory

2 cups (8 ounces) dried split
   fava beans
2 medium all-purpose potatoes,
   peeled and quartered

1 tsp. salt
1/2 cup extra-virgin olive oil
1 lb. chicory, stemmed, washed,
   and drained

Put fava beans and potatoes in a stockpot and cover with water. Add salt and bring to a boil. Boil uncovered for about 30 minutes, or until the beans are tender. Drain, reserving 1/4 cup of the cooking water.

Meanwhile, thoroughly wash and rinse chicory. Trim stems. In a heavy skillet, sauté chicory over medium heat, with no water or oil, until limp.

In a food processor puree the beans and potatoes with olive oil and the 1/4 cup

Joe Avelluto Jr. He and brother John operate Il Trullo, one of the best Italian restaurants in the Midwest.

cooking water until smooth. Transfer the puree to a saucepan. Over very low heat, stirring continuously, warm puree.

Arrange chicory on a serving platter. Spoon warm puree over the chicory. Drizzle with olive oil and serve

Asparagus Frittata

10-12 asparagus spears	3 tbsps. butter
1/4 cup extra-virgin olive oil	4 eggs
1/4 red onion sliced thin	Salt
2 cloves garlic, slivered	Freshly ground black pepper

In a medium-size ovenproof skillet, sauté the onion slices and asparagus in olive oil over medium high heat until both begin to brown. Reduce heat. Add garlic and butter. Cook for another 3-4 minutes.

In a small mixing bowl, beat eggs. Season with salt. Make sure asparagus spears are laying flat on the bottom of the skillet, then pour eggs over asparagus. Cook over medium low heat until eggs begin to set up around edges and edges can be lifted with a spatula.

Place skillet under broiler and let broil until eggs are completely set and beginning to brown. Remove to a serving platter.

The Avellutos. A well-fed family is a happy family.

Spaghetti with Zucchini and Red Potatoes

3 medium-size new red potatoes,
   peeled, halved and sliced
   1/2-inch thick
1 lb. spaghetti or spaghettini,
   broken into pieces about
   2 inches long

6-8 very small zucchini, sliced thin
1/3 cup extra-virgin olive oil
Freshly grated Parmesan cheese
Salt
Freshly ground black pepper

Cook spaghetti al dente in boiling salted water. Rinse in cold water, drain and set aside. In a heavy skillet, over medium-high heat sauté potatoes in oil until lightly browned and tender. Add zucchini and continue to cook until zucchini slices begin to turn translucent. Stir in spaghetti and let simmer until spaghetti is warm. Serve immediately with grated Parmesan cheese, salt and pepper to taste.

Lamb-Stuffed Prosciutto and Spinach Rolls

1 lb. ground lamb
6 cloves garlic, chopped fine
1/4 yellow onion, chopped fine
1 cup breadcrumbs
1/2 cup pitted Kalamata olives,
   chopped fine
1 egg, slightly beaten

2 tbsps. fresh lemon juice
Salt
Freshly ground pepper
24-30 large leaves fresh spinach,
   stemmed, washed and
   patted dry
12-18 large slices prosciutto

Preheat oven to 350 degrees. In a large mixing bowl combine the ground lamb, garlic, onion, breadcrumbs, olives, egg, and lemon juice. Season with salt and pepper to taste. Mix well with wooden spoon or by hand. Form 12-18 egg-shaped rolls with this meat mixture. Wrap each of these tightly in spinach leaves, covering completely. Then wrap each in one or two slices of prosciutto. Bake in a covered baking dish for 45 minutes to an hour, or until cooked through entirely. Serve with sour cream.

Fennel Potato Bake

2 lbs. new potatoes, scrubbed,
   peeled
2 bulbs fennel, roughly chopped
2 tbsps. fresh parsley, chopped
1/2 cup fresh basil, chopped
2 tbsps. extra virgin olive oil
4 yellow onions, chopped fine
2 cloves garlic, chopped fine

1/2 lb. mushrooms, sliced thin
Freshly ground black pepper
1/2 cup breadcrumbs
1 lb. fresh mozzarella cheese,
   sliced
Salt
Freshly ground pepper

Preheat oven to 400 degrees. Cut potatoes into 1/4-inch thick slices and cook in salted boiling water for about 15 minutes, until tender. Drain, and rice with a potato ricer. Cook fennel in salted boiling water for about 7 minutes, until tender, then drain. In a mixing bowl, combine and mix potatoes, fennel, parsley and basil.

In a heavy skillet, sauté onions until just beginning to caramelize. Add garlic and mushrooms and cook for another 2-3 minutes. Season with salt and pepper to taste.

Spread half the breadcrumbs on the bottom of a 9-by-9 baking dish. Spoon half the onion, garlic and mushroom mixture over the breadcrumbs. Cover with mozzarella slices. Spoon half the potato, fennel, parsley and basil mixture on top of the cheese. Add another layer of onions, garlic and mushrooms. Then another layer of cheese. Finish with a layer of potatoes. Spread the remaining breadcrumbs over the top. Bake for 20 minutes until golden brown. Serve warm.

Ricotta Pie

For the crust:
2 cups all-purpose flour	1/4 cup shortening
2-1/2 tsps. baking powder	2 eggs, lightly beaten
1/2 cup sugar	1 tsp. vanilla extract

In a large mixing bowl, combine flour, baking powder and half the sugar. Cut in the shortening and mix quickly and gently with your fingertips until the mixture resembles coarse crumbs. Add eggs and vanilla and quickly and gently work them into the dough. Divide dough into 2 balls and chill for at least 3-4 hours.

On a lightly floured work surface roll out one chilled dough ball into a disk to fit the bottom of the pie pan. Roll out the other ball of dough and cut into narrow strips about 1/2-inch wide to be used for the top crust.

For the filling:
1-1/2 lbs. ricotta cheese	1 cup sugar
6 eggs	1 tsp. vanilla extract
	1 tbsp. fresh grated lemon peel

In an electric mixer beat eggs, sugar, vanilla and lemon peel together. Fold in the ricotta cheese. Set aside.

Preheat oven to 325 degrees. Line greased pie pan with bottom pie crust. Pour filling into crust. Using a crisscross pattern lay dough strips across top. Trim overlap. Pinch edges where strips meet bottom crust. Cover edges with a strip of foil to prevent burning. Bake for 25 minutes. Remove foil and bake for another 25-30 minutes, or until an inserted knife comes out clean.

Index